According to Uffa

Handling Sailing Boats

ACCORDING TO UFFA

by

UFFA FOX

NEWNES : LONDON

First Published 1960

Text set 11 point Times New Roman, leaded 2 points
Printed in Great Britain by Cox & Wyman Ltd, London, Fakenham and
Reading, for George Newnes Limited, Tower House, Southampton Street,
London, W.C.2

Contents

CONTENTS

List of Plates

(*Photographs by Beken & Son, Cowes*)

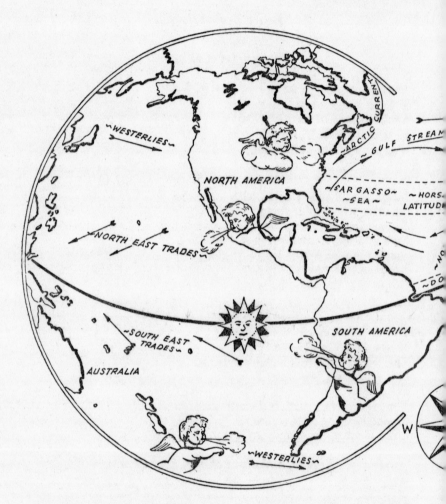

This map shows the main winds and some of the ocean currents of the
world. We see how the two great land masses running north and south

WESTERN HEMISPHERES

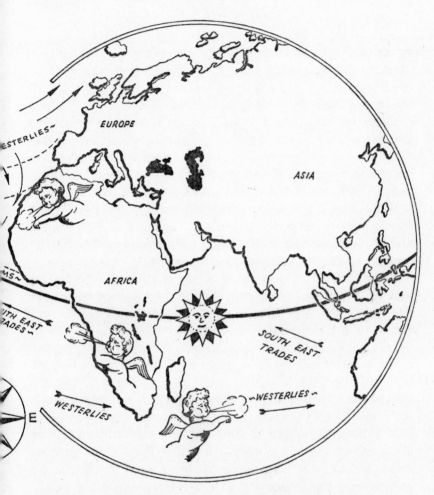

break up the Seven Seas, and how it is possible to use the winds and currents to get from place to place (see pages 13–17).

Introduction

THE Lord took six days only to make this wonderful earth of ours, and we mortals walk it for our allotted span of three score years and ten, all too few for us to appreciate and enjoy all its wonderful beauty of land, sky and sea.

Unless we have looked down from the summits of mountains and gazed in solitary thought down the deep valleys below; travelled over the hills and vales on foot or horse; descended into caves underground and been farmers and gardeners, we cannot have an understanding love and knowledge of the land.

Without having flown in aeroplanes or sailplanes we do not feel the majesty and power in clouds and up-currents of air rushing and lifting over hills and mountains, for when we are flying in the pure air we have a detached, ethereal feeling.

The old writers of hymns sang of heaven above the clouds, and how right they were. We, who often fly over Europe in autumn and winter, see their vision fulfilled, for then London, Paris and almost all of Europe is hidden for days at a time from the blue of the sky and the bright warmth of the sun. Yet this dreary, fog-like cloud is only a mile or so in height and once we pierce this, we burst out into brilliant sunshine and blue skies and now, from the sunshiny side, the dense cloud is a lovely, billowing white which is often level and looks as solid to walk upon as snow. Those who visit the mountain heights of Europe in winter are above all this low cloud and are inspired in body and soul by the glorious sunshine and so feel, as we do when suspended in air travel, that they are as near to being face to face with God as it is possible in this world.

Until we have swum in and under the sea we have no understanding of the wondrous realm of Neptune. We look up and the surface of the sea is a marvellous coverlet, with every shade of blue, green and white caused by ripples that constantly change their angles and facets. People derive pleasure from different facets of diamonds sending out beams of light, but the loveliness of sunlight striking down through the ruffled surface of the sea surpasses everything I know for inspiring beauty, far beyond the loveliness of light through the great cathedrals of Christendom, be they in London, Paris or Rome. Here, under the sea, we are with fishes, and as in an aeroplane we not only have movement ahead and sideways, but also up and down, and we can see all the plants on the rocks and sea-bed. To be at one with all the beauty of earth, sky and sea is at once the most exciting, inspiring and soothing of all human emotions.

This book is an attempt to help us all to enjoy the soul-satisfying pleasure of sailing the seas, lakes and rivers of this earth, traversing its wide waters without any noise except the clink, clink, clink of the waves and the swish of the seas as they are cleft by our vessel's cutwater. All the best things of this earth, such as the warmth of the sun, the freshness of the breeze, the mountain air, the rippling brook, are free. Once we have our sailing craft afloat it costs us nothing to sail: the wind, our driving power, is there whether we use it or not, as is the power and loveliness in the clouds, the mountain-torrents, rivers or streams. So, this book to teach you sailing is, as all these things, for your delight.

Sailing any one of the Seven Seas is a mysterious pleasure, for the fascination and fun of it are so great that they overcome the moments of misfortune and misery we must suffer at sea. We must know heartache to enjoy happiness, and know hunger to enjoy a meal, however good.

In contrasts we find fun. Watch any dog at home on a winter night. The library at my old home "Puckaster", on the under-cliff at the southern tip of the Isle of Wight, had three inside walls and with its great roaring log fire was the favourite room for the cold winter nights of January and February. Bruce, my Labrador, would lie near the fire till he panted from its heat, then he would go to the coldest corner of the room, cool off, and move once more to the fire to feel and enjoy its heat again. I taught him to stretch out where it was only pleasantly warm and he'd never have to move, but here there was no contrast, so no fun, and he would lie there only under orders—for his own enjoyment he continued to go from the heat of the fire to the cold of the corner.

Nowhere else do you get such contrasts as in sailing. A gale starts to brew: you see all the ominous signs in the sky a day before it starts to blow; you marvel at the might of the Lord and, filled with awe by the relentless power and majesty marching through the sky, have the fear of death and destruction on you for days. And then fair, favourable weather attends you and your heart is just as glad within you as it was distressed. This has been so from the beginning of time, and the purpose of this book is to enable you to enjoy sailing to the full without coming to any harm.

UFFA FOX

I

The Seven Seas and the Winds of Heaven

ONCE a man has tasted the salt brine of the open sea on his lips, he can never forsake it. The sea is his greatest benefactor, and at the same time a most exacting mistress. It brings tea from India and China, coffee from Brazil, cotton from America and Egypt, oranges and sherry from Spain, port from Portugal, wines from La Belle France—in fact the fruits from the uttermost ends of the earth—yet demands great attention, respect and knowledge, otherwise destruction awaits. Therefore, before we venture on wide and at times wild waters, we must understand the sea. First of all, he who would be a seaman must know the sea, its streams, drifts and currents, the winds that blow and what his ship will bear in fine and foul weather.

Seamen are fortunate not only in the fact that this earth of ours is three parts water, but also that the Seven Seas* have two great land masses, the continents of North and South America and Europe, Asia and Africa running north and south to divide them. Without these land masses it would be most dangerous to put to sea, as a tidal current would be sweeping round the Equator a thousand miles an hour.

The sea has a tidal range under the control of the moon because of its nearness to the earth, and to a lesser extent of the sun. Because the two masses of land run north and south, this tidal range is only a tidal wave, moving round the world without the particles of water moving, just as when you move your foot across the bed the clothes rise but remain stationary. Unless, of course, you are in one of those small, miserable beds where you never sleep because first of all the eiderdown slides off, then the bedclothes

* North and South Atlantic, North and South Pacific, Indian Ocean, Arctic Sea, Antarctic Sea.

escape from under the thin mattress so often that you battle with
the bed and never sleep a wink all night. However, suppose the
continents ran east and west—then, instead of the tidal wave,
there would be a current taken by the moon round the earth once
in every 24 hours and as the circumference at the Equator is
24,000 miles at this latitude the speed of this current would be,
1,000 m.p.h. Imagine this being opposed by a wind of 50 m.p.h.
and you have a picture of a sea no vessel could endure. No
oranges, no tobacco, no sailing to a warmer clime—the sea is now
a tyrant, not a benefactor.

The world at large is wonderfully planned and though, through
the ages, thousands of ships have sailed the sea, it has remained
unchanged for millions of years. Now, we move from the world
in general to one of the Seven Seas, in particular the North
Atlantic, so that we may more fully understand the way of the sea.

Its streams and drifts are fairly constant. The Equatorial current starts on the African coast just north of the Equator and flows
clear across the Atlantic at 30 to 60 miles a day until it reaches
the north coast of South America when it reaches its greatest
velocity of almost 100 miles a day. Then flowing into the Gulf of
Mexico it starts the warm Gulf Stream out on its long voyage
northwards up the American coast where it fans out from Greenland to Spain, its warm waters enabling palm trees and tropical
plants to grow on the south and west coasts of the British Isles
although the latitude is so high. From the west of Greenland the
cold Arctic current runs south past Newfoundland and Labrador
close to the North American coast and inside the Gulf Stream.
In June and July, when the ice breaks up in the Arctic, icebergs
are swept south by this current and, on meeting the warm Gulf
Stream off Newfoundland, they melt and deposit earth and moss,
thus forming the Grand Banks of Newfoundland and food for
the fish which all Europe has for many years sent vessels across the
Atlantic to catch. These icebergs meeting the Gulf Stream are
also the cause of this area having long periods of fog in June and
July, and of the dreadful loss of the *Titanic* in 1912 on her maiden
voyage and the loss of the Swedish ship *Alpha* in 1959, also on her
maiden voyage.

On the other side of the Atlantic, Renolds Current runs south across the Bay of Biscay, then doubles back westwards across the Atlantic through the North-East Trades to the Gulf of Mexico and starts on its circular tour of the Atlantic once again. The winds have a similar system. On the Equator there are the Doldrums, a belt of calms and variables ranging in extent from 100 miles in February to 300 miles in August. From Latitudes 8° to 27° there are the North-East Trades, where the wind blows regularly from the north-east year in year out, varying in strength from a fresh breeze to a gale and swinging two to three points in direction. Farther north, Latitudes 27° to 35° are the Horse Latitudes, with light, variable winds and fitful calms. Then from Latitudes 35° to 60° we have westerly winds ranging from light airs to gale force.

All this has been known for many years, and the old sailing ships on leaving the English Channel made Westing even with a fair wind lest the indraught and the prevailing Westerlies should drive them into the dreaded Bay of Biscay. Here we must remember that once the old square-rigged ships shortened sail, their enormous windage and the heavier seas now encountered prevented them from working out to windward and they feared greatly that they would be embayed, unable to weather the horns of the Bay. Moreover, the great Atlantic seas that have marched unhindered the full width of the Atlantic are now tripped up by the Continental Shelf as vessels come on soundings. From Longitude 10° to 12° W. these ships shaped a course to pass westward of Madeira and Cape Verde Islands, thus avoiding the heavy squalls and eddy winds to leeward of these islands. If bound round the Cape of Good Hope they steered to cross the Line between Longitude 23° and 29° W., sailing south through the North-East Trades they had to sail, as we do today, through the Doldrums, after which they met the South-East Trades and continued south.

A ship sailing to America, say as far as north as Halifax, by the southern route shaped her course to the west of Madeira, then, when well into the North-East Trades, ran westward till about Longitude 48° W., when she curved northwards, passing about 200 miles eastward of the Bermudas, allowing for the Gulf Stream setting across her course to the E.N.E. at anything from 20 to 70 miles a day. The old northern route was followed only

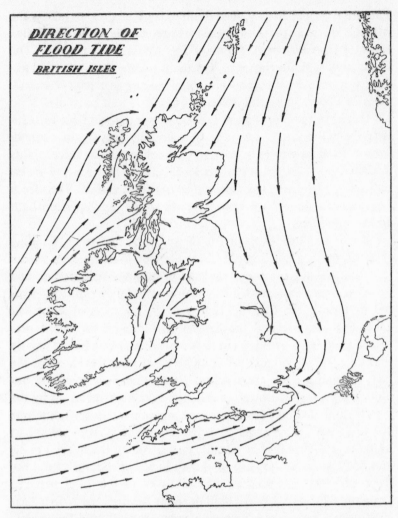

DIRECTION OF
FLOOD TIDE
BRITISH ISLES

This chart shows that the rising tide flows north-east on the west and south coasts and south down the east coast, meeting at Dover and Cape Wrath. Thus Grimsby, for example, can warn Great Yarmouth or London if there is a dangerously high tide on the way, and Plymouth can warn Southampton. The ebb naturally runs in the opposite direction to the flood, and both are affected by strong winds blowing with or against them.

If you are sailing from, say, Cowes to Grimsby, you try to take the flood tide up Channel as far as Dover and then the ebb tide up the North Sea; when making plans you find that a careful study of tide tables is invaluable.

in the autumn when it is free of icebergs. Once clear of the English Channel a course was shaped north-westward to Longitude 30° W. and Latitude 55° N., then south-westward for the Grand Banks of Newfoundland. Crossing the Banks in Latitude 47° 30″N. the lead was a sure guide for sounding the depths, while the thermometer also told of the approach to the Banks as the water temperature fell on leaving the warm Gulf Stream and entering the cold waters of the Arctic current. So the southern and northern routes were well known and much used. On the southern route ships were sometimes driven into the Horse Latitudes where there is neither wind nor current. The western half of this is called the Sargasso Sea, and I have spent days in this desolate part of the Atlantic surrounded by Gulf weed, without hope and sweaty hot, the sea teeming with fish of all kinds from minute crabs on the weed to great whales. The Sargasso is a place to avoid.

In the last fifty years the masting and rigging of vessels have improved so much that, though hull speeds have remained the same, light hollow spars and strong, small-diameter rigging have so reduced weight and windage aloft that it is now far quicker to sail directly across the Atlantic against the Westerlies and the Gulf Stream. All because of the wonderful, weatherly qualities of our present-day craft.

From the North Atlantic in general, we now turn to one particular place, the North Sea. If we look quietly at the chart of the North Sea, we discover truths that hold good the world over.

High land has deep water close inshore for, broadly speaking, the height of the land indicates the steepness of the slope of the beach. So the rule for sailing in countries like Scotland and Norway is to steer clear of everything you see and "all's well"; but you often have difficulty in finding a place to anchor, for the hills sweeping down almost plumb continue to do so under water and there is no bottom to be found on which the anchor can grip and hold. In complete contrast to this is the flat land of Holland and Norfolk at the southern end of the North Sea, for here the flat land runs out under the sea to form dangerous shoals well offshore.

Then, too, the North Sea has very troubled waters with a northerly wind, as the seas sweeping in at the wide entrance

B

between Norway and Scotland are restricted more and more as they race southwards, not only by the land closing in on either side but also by the rising sea-bed which shallows the water in the southern half. So the seas from the north are continually being tripped and tumbled and become dangerous as they race southward before a northerly gale. It is for the same reason that the Bristol Channel has such troubled waters, for even on the flood tide with a westerly wind, when wind and tide are together, these waters are turbulent.

Now we move to the smaller "Waters of the Wight", and by studying these we can understand all other waters, for they are at once both simple and complex. Simple in that, as in any other place on earth, the rise and fall of the tide as well as its direction and strength can be set out in tidal almanacs and charts, since tides are controlled by the moon and we know what the moon will be doing years ahead. Complex because the Isle of Wight stands boldly out into the English Channel to form a protecting breakwater for the great naval port of Portsmouth, and for Southampton, one of the chief shipping ports of the world. By jutting out into the main tidal stream, the Island causes a strange phenomenon: double high water at Southampton and various places on the Solent, as the last of the flood eddies round the eastern end of the Wight. The tide tables prepared by the Southampton Harbour Board give exact and precise information and show that whereas in nearly all places the tide ebbs and flows regularly, twice in every twenty-four hours, to give two high waters a day, Southampton has four high waters a day, a first and a second high water in each tide. The young flood rushes in to make the first high water, then ebbs a little and, after an hour or so, the main flood surges in to give the second high water. This was the undoing of the courtiers of King Canute in the days when, because of its central position in the south, Winchester was the seat of the Saxon and Danish Kings of England. The old fortified walled city of Southampton was the nearest seaport and stronghold. Canute's courtiers, knowing of this double tide and wishing to please their King, told him that even the sea would obey him. Now either the candles they used for time burnt slowly, or the mead was so good they lingered long or they had slow horses—

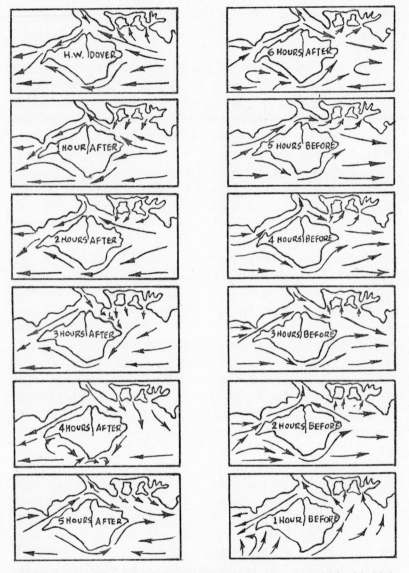

Isle of Wight Tidal Charts: These charts show why there is double high water in the Solent; it is caused by eddy running round the east end of the island.

anyway, when they set the King's chair on the Southampton strand, instead of the young flood and the first high water ebbing, the main flood was setting in and King Canute got wet feet.

A study of the set of twelve-hourly charts of the Wight tells us where the tidal streams run regularly year in and year out, all given from the time of high water. The time of high water is set out for the year in all nautical almanacs, or if we have no nautical almanac, we have only to remember that it is high water at Cowes at 10.45 a.m. at the full and new moon (full and change), that the west-going (ebb) stream starts one and a half hours before high water at Cowes and runs westward for six hours, and the east-going or flood stream runs for six hours. We can then work from this, adding twenty minutes on each tide. Every flood and ebb tide takes twelve hours and twenty minutes to run, so that with two tides to be fitted into every twenty-four hour day each tide is approximately three-quarters of an hour later than the last.

So far, we have considered only the rise and fall of the tide, but you cannot have this without an ebb and flow of the tidal streams and these vary in strength from 1 to 6 miles an hour round the Isle of Wight and up to 10 miles an hour in such places as the Pentland Firth in the North of Scotland. Those tides that march in easterly and westerly directions are fiercer than those that travel on northerly and southerly courses because the earth in its orbit travels from west to east. The flood tide in the English Channel runs eastward from Land's End towards Dover and the ebb tide westward. A glance at the tidal charts for the Island reveals that where outside, at the back of the Wight and also in the Solent from the Needles to Cowes, the flood runs east and the ebb west, this is not so at the east end. From Bembridge Ledge to Cowes the last half of the flood and the last of the ebb run in the opposite direction to the main Channel tide, and it is this that gives Southampton its double high water. Only on the young flood and the first of the ebb is it in unison with the English Channel.

Very few know of the historical interest of Southampton, but in addition to its close association with King Canute, it is also connected with Winchester which some people think was King Arthur's Camelot, and where his reputed Round Table still rests. So the walled and well-fortified Southampton, only twelve miles south, was naturally his seaport, Winchester and Southampton being the scene of this poem which, handed down through the ages, sheds an interesting light on those far-off days:

In ancient times when Arthur bold was King
Honour and chivalry were all the thing,
With certain reservations as the Dames
Were not averse to fun and games.
Hence the bold knight departing for the wars
Locked up his ladye love in metal drawers.

So good King Arthur, setting sail for France,
With Guinevere refused to take a chance,
And as he placed his fond Adieus upon her lips
She felt the chill of steel upon her hips.
Fainting she fell recumbent from the shock:
On went the pants and click went the lock.

Sir Lancelot, the Captain of the L.D.V.s,
Was stretched full length reclining at his ease,
When to the Knight's surprise the King threw him the key:
"Guard it, Sir Knight, and all temptations spurn,
"Then three years hence and failing my return,
    "It's yours for keeps."

The Knight arose and pressed his sword hilt to his lips;
The King rode forth in splendour to his ships.

But as the fleet was getting under way
A wild commotion stirred the Bay.
A knight—Sir Lancelot—galloped madly on the shore:
"Stop, stop, Good King," called he,
"You've given me the wrong confounded key."
To which the King replied, "You're telling me!"

Then close outside the old city walls stands the statue to John Alden and the *Mayflower* for, whereas most people think she sailed from Plymouth, Southampton was her starting port. She only called at Plymouth on her way. And it was from Cowes that two ships,

the *Ark* and the *Dove*, sailed under the Earl of Baltimore to found
the State of Maryland in America. All these ships worked exactly
the same tides as we do today. The tides round the Island run
faster in the deep-water Channel and less inshore. In bays there
is generally a back eddy and this holds true all over the world,
not only for tidal waters but also for rivers and streams. The Solent
tides generally run at 3 to 4 knots and increase to 6 knots through
the Narrows of Hurst, the Needles, and St Catherines Race, as
here the same amount of water has to pass a confined space in
the same time. So, just as rivers have "rapids" when restricted,
tidal streams have "races".

Shakespeare causes Caesar, who lived in a land-locked and
therefore tideless sea, to say an unnatural but nevertheless a true
thing: "We must take the current when it serves or lose our ven-
tures." Perhaps Caesar had studied the tides of Calais and Dover,
but certainly he was right.

A boat sailing at 6 knots *against* a 4-knot tide, only travels at
2 knots over the ground; but sailing at 6 knots *with* a 4-knot tide
she covers the ground at 10 knots, a difference of 8 knots made
good. So the importance of tide is double that first supposed. A
boat can only sail within 45° of the wind, so beating to windward
with her sails pinned in tight she can only sail at a speed equal to
the square root of her waterline length. Suppose her to have a
25-ft. waterline, then her speed is 5 knots. As she zigzags her way
to windward her speed made good through the water directly to
windward is only 4 knots; against the 4-knot tide her speed is zero,
but with it, it is 8 knots. So Shakespeare is right again when he
makes Caesar say: "It boots us ill to resist both wind and tide."

The waters inside the Wight are as fascinating, interesting and
historical as any in the world, as well as being the safest on which
to learn to sail, whether racing or cruising. There are little harbours every four miles, so that with no wind and a fair tide they
are only approximately one hour apart while, with a fair wind and
tide, less than half an hour apart—a perfect place for beginners
and experts.

Cowes, in the centre, can be entered at all states of the tide and,
since between Whitsun and September the prevailing winds are
southerly and westerly, it affords perfect shelter and means that

you approach into wind and so can stop easily. On entering, the Castle, passed to starboard, was built by Henry VIII and houses the Royal Yacht Squadron, the premier club of the world. Within 150 yards is the Royal London Yacht Club, with the cannon used by Nelson at Teneriffe, the Royal Corinthian Yacht Club, with its lawn and large dining-room, and the Island Sailing Club, with its 3,000 members and launch service. There are also the East Cowes, Cowes Corinthian and Gurnard Sailing Clubs. To port, surrounded by trees, can be seen East Cowes Castle, once the home of John Nash who designed Buckingham Palace, Regent Street and Carlton House Terrace, and who now sleeps peace-fully with his wife close to the west door of East Cowes church. The local hospital was once a seaman's home designed for and given in memory of Lindsay James, its weathervane being a lovely model of his famous *Lancashire Witch* that knew the Arctic as well as the tropics. Close at hand is Osborne House, once the home of Queen Victoria. But more important than all this to a yachtsman is Captain George Barton, the Harbour Master. He has mooring facilities for 500 yachts, and as the charter of the Cowes harbour commissioners does not allow them to make a profit, moorings are at their bare cost. In consequence, they are in great demand and difficult to obtain.

Every little harbour has its interest as well as the fun of entering. Newtown, four miles west, whose waters are still pure enough for oyster beds, has one of the oldest Town Halls of England and a wonderful variety of birds: Arctic terns, oyster catchers, nightin-gales, in fact practically every British bird except the bittern. Yar-mouth, another four miles west, is a snug and friendly harbour with a castle built by Henry VIII, and a statue of Louis XIV in its church which is pure delight. Then, under the shadow of the white cliffs of the Needles there are Totland and Colwell bays, sheltered from the north by the shingle bank.

On the north shore Hurst Castle, another built by Henry VIII to guard the Narrows inside which lay Keyhaven, Lymington and Beaulieu Rivers, all set in the New Forest each and every one with an interest and a charm of its own. The old shipyard of Beaulieu used to build our wooden walls, and its old Abbey brings peace to the mind. Farther along is Calshot Castle, again built

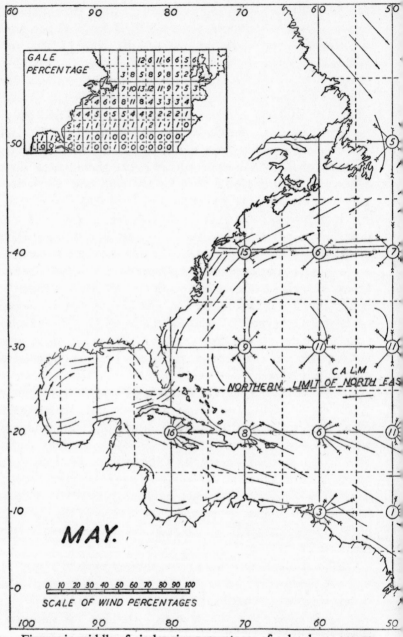

Figures in middle of circles give percentages of calm days; arrows
give wind directions; lengths of arrows (measured on scale at bottom
left) give percentages of winds; barbs on arrows give wind force (on
Beaufort Scale); small chart at top left gives percentages of gales.

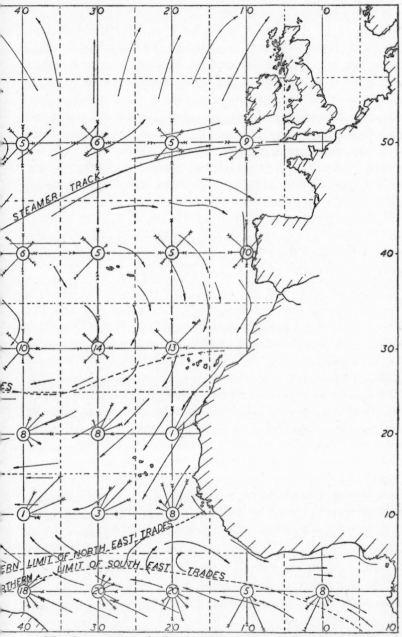

The long arrows indicate ocean currents. The Steamer Track takes ships well south of the fogs on the Newfoundland banks where the Arctic current runs into the Gulf Stream.

by Henry VIII who is remembered only by his various wives, yet was in fact one of the most wonderful kings England ever had. These four castles on a twelve-mile stretch of water tell of his plans for our defence, and he improved our fighting ships so that they could sail within 5 points of the wind. Even today we can only sail within 4 points in spite of our modern fore and aft rig, and we do not have to carry cannons and cannon balls. As well as all this he was a great designer of cannon, and at Southampton there is still preserved a bronze cannon given by him to the town. His navy could outsail and outrange anything in the world and it was his ships and cannon, as used by the Elizabethan seamen, which saved us from the Spanish Armada when it came, filled with soldiers and determined on victory by storming and boarding. But our men, outranging and outmetalling the Spaniards as well as outsailing them, kept them within range of our cannon while keeping our own ships out of range of the Spanish.

Then, there is the eastern arm of the Solent with Portsmouth, Nelson's flagship *Victory*; Bembridge, its lobsters and prawns; Seaview and Wootton Creek and Kings Quay, all full of sailing vessels as well as beauty and historical interest. Then, when we have learnt the inside of the Wight, we can venture out into the Channel and beyond, to France, Spain, Portugal, in fact anywhere on the Seven Seas, provided we have the time and a sturdy, well-found ship. And I would put the smallest sensible vessel as one with a 24-ft. waterline, for it is impossible to get full headroom below this length.

Tides

We must remember that the tidal wave, a rise and fall in height of water, and the tidal stream, are separate and distinct, some places in fact having a tidal wave but little or no tidal stream. The reason we must keep these separate in our mind is that at Cowes the west-going or ebb stream starts $1\frac{1}{2}$ hours before high water and the east-going or flood stream starts $1\frac{1}{2}$ hours before low water, which shows how important it is to keep these two separate and distinct in our mind.

All charts are marked with depths of water or heights of banks above the average low-water level, and this is called Mean Low

Water of Ordinary Spring Tides. So for navigation we must look at the height of the tide, as often we can save miles by sailing over banks when the tide is high enough; then for position we must make allowances for the tidal stream, as its effect is double its speed, when with or against us. So both height of tide and speed of the tidal stream are of the utmost importance to us. Fortunately all this is predicted for us in the nautical almanacs, so while we do not know what the wind and weather will do, we do know what the tides are doing at any hour of the day and night throughout the year. But due allowance must be made for the effect of strong weather on tides. Heavy gales blowing with the run of the flood tide will increase the height of the tide and the speed of the tidal stream. If they blow against the flood, the tidal stream will decrease both in height and in current, naturally increasing the ebb, so that the depth of water at low tide will be less than predicted.

The moon—and, to a lesser extent, the sun—controls our tides, and at every full and new moon, called "—full" and "change" in nautical almanacs, the tides have the greatest range. They are then higher and also lower, and this in turn, makes the tidal currents run faster. At the Equinoxes—around the 21st of March and September—we have the greatest tidal rise and fall of the year, for then the sun and moon are not only in unison but on these days the sun crosses the Line (the Equator) and produces equal day and night all over the world.

Tides can be a great hindrance or a great help. In the English Channel the flood and ebb streams change every six hours, but we can work a nine-hour fair tide and have only three hours against us in every twelve hours if we are beating to the west against the prevailing wind. The tide is always weakest inshore and its direction inshore changes 1½ hours earlier than offshore. Therefore, when going westward and beating to windward, we stand offshore to take the last of the west-going stream and hold off for 1½ hours after the stream has turned, then tack for the shore and, standing close in, we work almost a nine-hour fair tide and have only a three-hour foul tide. There is a certain period of slack water, and even when the tide turns it takes some time to gather momentum and strength.

As the tide generally runs fastest in the deep channels, when it is with you, you keep to the centre of the river, estuary or channel, and when it is against you, to the bank or shore where it will be less and turns earliest in your favour. Here, too, you will often find an eddy tide in your favour. In the English Channel the average rise and fall is 7 ft. and the speed of the stream, flood and ebb, an average of 2½ knots. This speed is increased at headlands as all the water of the bays, being constricted by the points, must go past in the same time and has to accelerate to do so. Therefore we must beware of all headlands—such as Portland Bill, where we have a stream of 6 knots going over a rough, uneven bottom causing a wild and confused sea leaping up and exploding. We should carefully study all headlands, not only for the strength of the tide, but for the state of the water which at times can be rough enough to overwhelm a vessel. Tidal streams and currents at sea, in estuaries and rivers are alike in that on the edges the current is less as the water is shallowest. The old saying "still waters run deep" tells us this, for under a calm surface the powerful river current runs relentlessly and seemingly placidly in the deep water channel. In the shallows, though it may be noisy and turbulent, it runs less swiftly and this is the course which fish and boats follow when making a passage up against the stream. So when we have a fair stream we keep well out and curve round the points and headlands in the strength of the stream; when the stream is against us we follow the shore, traversing the shallows that have enough water for us.

All places have a Tidal Constant given in pilot books and on charts at the full and change of the moon or, as we express it ashore, full and new moon. At Cowes on full and change days the first highwater is 10.45 and the second is at 11.45, the springs rise about 12½ ft. and the neaps 9½ ft., the tide flowing into the harbour seven hours and ebbing five hours. The tidal range varies in height and strength round the Wight. At the Needles springs rise 6½ ft. and neaps 5 ft. and the speed of the stream in the Needles Channel varies between 4 and 3 knots and south of the Needles in the English Channel it drops to 2 knots. In the Narrows of Hurst the speed is 6 to 5 knots. North of the Shingle Bank the tidal stream is less—only 2½ to 1 knot. Through the Solent,

from Cowes to Hurst, the stream runs at 3 to 2 knots, and in
Spithead Cowes to Bembridge 2½ to 1½ knots, as the waters are
wider here. But all these tidal streams vary with the weather. I
have known the flood driven before a heavy south-westerly gale
prevent the pilot-cutter from battling her way out through the
Narrows of Hurst, in spite of her ability to steam 10 knots in quiet
weather.

At the back of the Wight the tidal streams are easier as this is the
open Channel except for St Catherine's Point. Here we have a
violent race on the flood and ebb, for all the waters of the Bay to
the west and east must run past this Headland on the flood and ebb.
So with about three times the volume to pass, the speed is trebled
and the waters become turbulent. This is the rule of all coasts,
rivers and estuaries. Whenever the stream is constricted it must
accelerate in proportion to the amount it is confined, as the same
amount of water has to pass in the same time.

The Winds of Heaven

A seaman's life is entirely dependent on the winds of heaven, on
their direction, strength and characteristics, and it is significant
that when the compass came from that old civilisation, the Chinese,
to the cradle of European navigation, the Mediterranean, all its
points except two, north and east, were named after the winds of
the Mediterranean Sea. The early European compass was made
for the Mediterranean where north points to La Belle France and
so it is that the heraldic emblem of France, the *fleur de lis*, marked,
and still marks to this day, the north point of the compass. Then,
because of the deep religious fervour, a cross marked the east and
continued to do so on English compasses until 1760. Even today,
the compass in France is called *La Rose des Vents* and in Spain,
Rosa de los Vientos. On the floor of the roof garden over "The
Commodores' House", my home at Cowes, I have painted a
facsimile of the first compass of Europe to remind me forever
that winds rule a sailor's life and that the compass is his unerring
guide.

There has been no change in wind and weather or the sea itself
for thousands of years, and once in every five or so years, we get
such a year as 1588 when the Spanish Armada attempted to invade

England. While the ships of the Armada were sailing from the south to assemble off the north-west corner of Spain at Ferrol and Corunna, their captains recorded weather and westerly gales as heavy as in mid-winter. The Armada arrived off south-west England late in July, right in the middle of our south-west monsoon, and swept up-Channel before the prevailing south-westerlies. Meanwhile the beacon fires had warned England from Land's End to Dover and London, and while Drake's advisers wished him to put to sea immediately, he wisely finished his game of bowls as, had he sailed then, he would have been to leeward of the Spaniards. As it was, he kept between them and Plymouth to defend it, and then sailed out to sea behind and to windward of the great Armada. As this proceeded majestically up-Channel he sailed to and fro across the enemy sterns pouring in shot after shot, and though they replied, it was useless, as Drake was using the cannons of Henry VIII which outranged all other guns on earth. He was, moreover, sailing the ships developed by Henry VIII, which could sail within 5 points of the wind and so he could both outsail and outrange the Spanish ships. Off the Isle of Wight, Drake was reinforced with ships and, although he was still greatly outnumbered, the running fight continued.

Count Medina Sidonia wished only to capture Plymouth as a base, and also the Isle of Wight, but he sailed past without attempting either, although at this stage his Armada was almost intact. And so they came to the Straits of Dover, where the English fleet was further reinforced so that it equalled the Spaniards in numbers but outmetalled and outranged them with its guns. After fire ships had disturbed the Armada our fleet went in at close range and with their heavier cannons and shot wrought such havoc that the Armada could not possibly beat westward down-Channel and so drove northwards round Scotland and home, less than half reaching sunny Spain. I have always admired this Armada for, after sailing into a sullen, cold and relentless sea, and enduring such a battering, not one ship surrendered. Such was their courage.

When it was all over Queen Elizabeth I struck a medal which said (in Latin): "God blew with his wind and they were scattered."

More than two hundred years later Nelson, as he lay dying in

Victory's cockpit, cried: "Anchor, Hardy, anchor! . . . do you anchor, Hardy?" Captain Hardy then said: "Shall we make the signal, sir?" "Yes," answered Nelson, "for if I live, I'll anchor." Nelson's last command was an entreaty, and coming from our greatest seaman and fighter, whose foresight and judgment were never at fault, it should have been carried out, for had his dying command and wish been obeyed we should have had nineteen prizes at Trafalgar instead of only four. The rest foundered or were driven ashore by the gale that came on. Nelson, with his seaman's instinct, knew that a westerly gale was brewing, and that our fighting ships and prizes would have so much of their rigging shot away that they could never hold off the shore by sailing. It is a known fact that once these ships shortened sail they did not make an inch to windward because of their enormous windage.

Broadly speaking, the weather in a certain country is much the same year after year, and the climate in the British Isles is fairly constant and true, though we do get the odd years, perhaps one in seven, when the run of weather is different.

January, February, March, April and early May are of course cold months. The Atlantic being warmer than the snow and ice-bound land mass of Europe and Asia, the winds are generally north-easterly with, of course, south-westerly gales breaking through in between. In April the wind is still north-easterly, but less severe, although we do get heavy north-easterly gales sometimes in this month. May and June are fairly quiet months for wind and now the sun has come north of the line and is starting to heat up this land mass. By the middle of July the whole of Europe and Russia has heated up and starts sucking in wind from the broad Atlantic. This wind, south-westerly in direction, comes in with great clouds that lift over the land and then start raining on it. And so from the middle of July to the end of August our south-west monsoon is reigning, and you have periods of a week or ten days with strong sou'-westers swinging to the north-west and then repeating this cycle over and over again. These figures are not exact, but broadly speaking for a week we have twelve hours of south-west wind and rain, then the wind swings west or north-west, blowing the same strength, but out of a bright clear sky. Then there is perhaps a lull of a week and this will be repeated again. By the end of August the days have started to get shorter, some of the power has gone out of the sun, and the south-west monsoon has cooled off the land mass, and so September finds us with gentle and light north-easterly breezes. October, November, December, bring in great westerlies again, some north and some south, all mixed together. That is the broad pattern of our year and it has been going on like this since the beginning of time.

People who take their holidays in August always complain of the bad summer weather, because they have lived in cities out of sight of the sky, sun, moon and stars, and entirely forget that the loveliness of the weather in May and June has enough rain in it to make anyone not noticing think that it is always raining, and they only remember the south-west monsoon of August. The summer of 1959, however, was an exception. A most wonderful summer. On the night of Friday, July 10th, there was a great thunderstorm. And the following day the wind had changed from east to south-west and was blowing a summer gale. In fact, it was blowing so hard that the Committee stopped the race after only one round and both my crew and I, who were racing the Duke of Edinburgh's *Coweslip*, had agreed as we were sailing up to the line that we had no desire or zest for another round like that.

Next day, Sunday the 12th, there was a race for the Princess Elizabeth Cup, presented by Her Majesty the Queen, and we were in the 40-ton cutter, *Drumbeat*. Everyone came to the line reefed and the 12-meter *Kaylena* revelled in this long, hard drive to windward, and was soon out into first place, while we in *Drumbeat*, with a smallish jib and a well-reefed mainsail, were in second place. All went well with us for the first round, but on the second round as we were approaching the West Bramble buoy, with no margin under our lee, two huge waves following each other pushed us to leeward, and just touching the buoy we had to retire. After this we had another four days of strong Westerlies, but because the land was so dry there was no rain with them. Then once again the wind swung back and continued blowing gently from the east against all the laws of life until Sunday the 26th. Then, late in the day, came another thunderstorm, and once again the wind swung into the west, so that the Monday's Dragon Race for the Duke of Edinburgh's Cup was sailed in a strong south-westerly wind. And with the heavy clouds marching across the sky without rain, it looked as if at last the south-west Monsoon was about to assert itself in spite of being one week late. But it was not so, and it never came in till the end of the Fastnet Race and then only half-heartedly.

The least variation in wind strength or direction makes all the difference in the world to life in a sailing boat. With little or no wind life is quiet but tedious aboard, for trying to sail is just like trying to hold a skating championship without ice. With winds from 5 to 15 m.p.h. we have perfect conditions for sailing. From 15 to 20 m.p.h. it starts to get a little strenuous, and though racing vessels carry full sail in winds up to 25 m.p.h., the cruisers generally start to shorten sail at 20. That is a difference between racing and cruising. In racing you reef so that your boat is travelling at her top speed in the lulls and wildly overpowered in the squalls, whereas when cruising you reef till your boat is comfortable in the squalls and undercanvassed in the lulls. It is for this reason that cruising men cannot understand why the racing boat is almost always being driven harder than the cruising boat, and this is also the reason why the rigging in racing boats is as a general rule better kept than that of a cruiser. The reverse should be the rule, as the racer, if he loses his mast or has an accident of any kind, always has another racing boat close at hand to render assistance if required, whereas the cruiser is generally ploughing a lonely furrow in search of peace and solitude with no one at hand to help if his rigging is carried away. So that if he loses his mast with a rock-bound shore to leeward, he is in distress.

Many people talk about the moon affecting the weather. Actually the moon controls only the tides; if it affected the weather, a nautical almanac could be written giving wind direction and strength as well as the tidal times and heights. So we can discount all talk of the moon controlling the weather or the tides controlling the weather, and look for other factors.

My belief is that just as the heating-up and cooling-off of the great land mass of Europe and Russia affects the wind over a large area, so this is also true of England and all islands. In fine, settled weather England is heated up during the day, air is sucked in off the sea to fill the "vacuum" caused by the hot air rising off

c

the land, and at night when the land cools down the air is then sucked from the land on to the sea, and you have a day (sea) and night (land) breeze, exactly as in the Mediterranean in settled weather.

In fine, calm weather on the Solent, we wake up in the morning with a light north-easterly breeze (the land breeze) and a clear sky, and then start looking northwards over England for what we call the "little messengers" and about 11 o'clock in the morning there can be seen over England the little white clouds at the top of the rising currents. And these "little messengers" tell us who look for them that by 1.00 British Summer Time the easterly wind will die away and a south-wester start to pull in and that this will develop into a smart breeze of 18 or 20 m.p.h., perhaps more. We also know that when the cool of the evening arrives this breeze will die away, so that by 7.00 it is a gentle breeze, and at 8.00 in the evening there is hardly any left. Then, as the land cools off, a light north-east wind will pull off the land and out into the Channel.

This knowledge helps wise sailing committees to postpone an important race from 11.00 to 1.30 in the afternoon, and enables those taking part in a race that cannot be postponed to prepare for this calm patch followed by the complete change of wind. I well remember racing in *Endeavour* with Sir T. O. M. Sopwith and winning a King's Cup Race because we knew of this change from east to west, and that it would take place about 1.15. So we were all ready for it, and glided out of a light easterly with a spinnaker set to a sparkling south-wester smoothly and swiftly with our spinnaker down and our headsails, that had been set up in stops, already broken out in a twinkling of an eye. No one else in that race was ready for this and so we sailed swiftly away from the fleet into an ever-increasing south-wester that continually widened our lead. There are, of course, days when you misjudge the weather, but thank goodness, we forget those quickly and easily, just as we do our aches and pains directly we are well again.

A study of the wind and weather is not only useful but continually lifts our eyes to the loveliness of the heavens, the wonderful blue in the sky, the marvellous patterns of the sunshine and shadow in clouds and of clouds racing past the moon. All this

Weather Report Divisions: The British Isles weather reports cover an area measuring 2,000 miles from north to south and 1,000 miles from east to west. Seamen pay attention to the report not only for their own area but also for areas to windward, so that they know in good time what is coming their way.

beauty has a peaceful, soothing and inspiring effect on our minds and bodies. For the seaman's motto when hoisting or lowering sails—"Always look aloft"—is true of our daily lives whether ashore or afloat, and I am always astonished when I go to London town to find how seldom you see people looking up at the sky. If only they would, it would lift them out of the dreariness of their surroundings. So on your way through life, "Always look aloft".

Today, we have weather ships stretched across the Atlantic, aeroplanes sending in meteorological knowledge, and several times during the twenty-four hours in each day many weather reports are broadcast. Such is the extent of this information and knowledge that these weather forecasts cover an area from Iceland to Finisterre, and from Norway out to Rockall in the Atlantic, an area oblong in shape some two thousand miles north and south and one thousand miles in its east and west direction, extending three hundred miles north, south, east and west of the British Isles. This great area is sub-divided again into areas with such euphonious names to a seaman's ear as Plymouth, Portland, Wight, Dogger, Faroes, Iceland, Rockall, Shannon and Finisterre, each one with its own particular weather report.

Those of us who have listened to these weather reports and forecasts have not only derived much knowledge from them, but also a great deal of fun. For in the war, when London was being bombed, I well remember one six-o'clock weather forecast during a cold winter spell describing all the various degrees of frost that would be experienced in these different areas and finally the Announcer with a chuckle ended up: "And we advise all those with brass monkeys to take them indoors tonight." For it was indeed what seamen call "brass monkey weather". On another occasion the Announcer, all innocently, said there would be "shattered scowers".

Weather reports, like every other prophecy, cannot always be true, for sometimes, although carefully plotted and tracked, weather and storms change their direction; but in the main these reports are trustworthy and a great guide, not only to seamen but also to farmers.

We can often look up into the sky and see clouds at different heights travelling in differing directions, and although these clouds look very remote, none of them is more than seven miles high; for that is the maximum height of clouds and something like eight to ten miles the maximum height of the weather. And so weather deals with an area all over the world some seven miles in height beyond which there is no weather. After that, you are up in the cloudless, limitless blue.

BROAD OUTLINE OF WINDS

NORTH ATLANTIC

DOLDRUMS	calm variable EQUATOR to 8° N.
NORTH-EAST TRADES	8° N. to 27° N.
HORSE LATITUDES	calm variable 27° N. to 35° N.
ANTI-TRADES WESTERLY WINDS	35° to 60° N.
S.-W. MONSOON	C. Roxo to C. Palmas and as far out as 32° W. July, August and September.

ENGLISH CHANNEL

EASTERLIES	January to May and September.
VARIABLE	Middle May to middle July.
S.-W. MONSOON	Middle of July to end of August.
STRONG WESTERLY	October, November, December and breaking through the easterlies of January, February and March.

MEDITERRANEAN

PONENTE (West)	General.
LEVANTE (East)	March, July, August.
SIROCCO (South-East)	Summer.
GREGALES (North-East)	Winter.

TABLE OF CHANGE IN COMPASS
DIRECTIONS THROUGH THE AGES

LA ROSA *32 Winds Italian*	BOUSSOLE *32 Points French*	COMPASS *32 Points English*	COMPASS *360 Degrees English*
TRAMONTANA	*NORD*	*NORTH*	*0*
4.Tramontana Greco	Nord 1/4 Nord-Est	North by East	11 1/4
Tramontana Greco	Nord Nord-Est	North North East	22 1/2
Greco Tramontana	Nord Est 1/4 Nord	North East by North	33 3/4
Greco	*Nord-Est*	*North East*	*45*
Di Greco Levante	Nord-Est 1/4 Est	North East by East	56 1/4
Levante Greco	Est Nord-Est	East North East	67 1/2
4.Di Levante Greco	Est 1/4 Nord-Est	East by North	78 3/4
LEVANTE	*EST*	*EAST*	*90*
Di Levante Sirocco	Est 1/4 Sud-Est	East by South	101 1/4
Levante Sirocco	Est Sud-Est	East South-East	112 1/2
4.Di Sirocco Levante	Sud-Est 1/4 Est	South East by East	123 3/4
Sirocco	*Sud-Est*	*South East*	*135*
4.Di Sirocco Ostro	Sud-Est 1/4 Sud	South East by South	146 1/4
Ostro Sirocco	Sud Sud-Est	South South East	157 1/2
4.Di Ostro Sirocco	Sud 1/4 Sud-Est	South East by South	168 3/4
OSTRO	*SUD*	*SOUTH*	*180*
4.Di Ostro Garbino	Sud 1/4 Sud-Ouest	South by West	191 1/4
Ostro Garbino	Sud Sud-Ouest	South South West	202 1/2
4.Di Garbino Ostro	Sud-Ouest 1/4 Sud	South West by South	213 3/4
Garbino	*Sud-Ouest*	*South West*	*225*
4.Di Garbino Ponente	Sud-Ouest 1/4 Ouest	South West by West	236 1/4
Ponente Garbino	Ouest Sud-Ouest	West South West	247 1/2
Di Ponente Garbino	Ouest 1/4 Sud-Ouest	West by South	258 3/4
PONENTE	*OUEST*	*WEST*	*270*
4.Di Ponente Maestro	Ouest 1/4 Nord-Ouest	West by North	281 1/4
Ponente Maestro	Ouest Nord-Ouest	West North West	292 1/2
Di Maestro Ponente	Nord-Ouest 1/4 Ouest	North West by West	303 3/4
Maestro	*Nord-Ouest*	*North West*	*315*
4.Di Maestro Tramontana	Nord-Ouest 1/4 Nord	North West by North	326 1/4
Tramontana Maestro	Nord Nord-Ouest	North North West	337 1/2
4.Di Tramontana Maestro	Nord 1/4 Nord-Ouest	North by West	348 3/4
TRAMONTANA	*NORD*	*NORTH*	*360*

II

Your First Boat

FIRST a child crawls, then totters and stumbles along, finally runs, skips and jumps. And so we should first learn to sail in a non-capsizing boat, then go on to sail boats that capsize, for the more exciting the craft the more easily she is likely to capsize. Speed is only obtained at the expense of safety.

Keel boats—vessels with ballast keels fixed on to their bottoms —are non-capsizing and therefore ideal boats to learn to sail in, as all our attention can be devoted to learning and understanding the mystery and magic of sea, sky, wind and sailing. There are hundreds of boats to choose from, but best of all is a one-design boat, because you are not yet designing a dream boat of your own, but learning to sail. One-designs have these advantages: their price is stable, many people as well as the designer have approved their hull and rig, the parts are standardised, as is the hull and gear, so that replacement of parts or of a complete vessel is easy.

And there are many owners of similar boats who will always be delighted to help with advice if asked—and even if not asked. You can find information about many of them in my last book, *Sailing Boats*.*

One of the Flying Family is the best one-design of the keel classes for the "new entry", because they have independent keels and rudders and extremely light displacement which gives them the characteristics of drop-keel craft without their capsizing tendency. They also cost less than other keel boats. For two children up to sixteen years of age the Flying Ten at £185 is ideal. For a parent and child or two lightweights the Flying Twelve at £265 is the boat. A man from far-away Australia asked me to design him

* George Newnes Ltd.

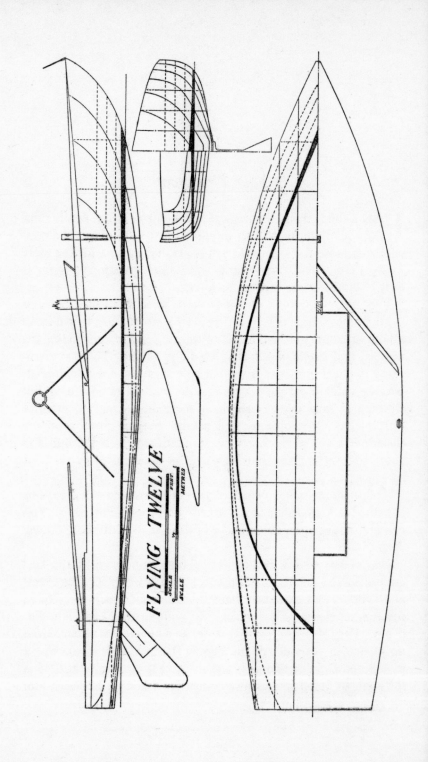

FLYING TWELVE

SCALE OF FEET

SCALE OF METRES

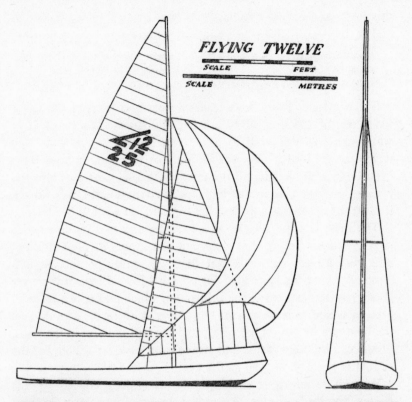

Sail Plan: The sails are low and snug for hard driving, the mainsail luff being only twice as long as the main boom. Only one forestay and a pair of mainshrouds are allowed—a simple, strong and effective rig.

(*Left*) **Lines:** These lines show the V'd sections going down to a deep chest forward and gradually flattening as they go aft, still keeping the wedge shape so that the harder the vessel is driven the more she lifts out of the water. The iron fin keel is widest at the bottom to give the vessel stability and also to make a flat base for her to stand on.

this boat, and having a ballast keel she is safe to learn sailing in and is, moreover, cheap to build and maintain.

Length Overall: 16′ (4·876m)	*Length Waterline:* 12′ (3·657 m)
Beam: 4′ 7″ (1·397m)	*Draught:* 2′ (·609m)
Displacement: 650 lb. (295 kilos)	*Sail Area:* 140 sq. ft. (13 sq. m)

She is a light, lively, uncapsizable boat and because she has a fixed keel of 255 lb. underneath her and draws only two feet of water, there is little need for this to be hoisted or lowered. The weight of the hull is only 112 lb. and she has planing lines. This little boat, while having all the safety of a keel boat, has also the planing performance of our high-speed centreboard boats, so she is ideal for those who like exciting fun and yet wish to be safe.

The mast is quite simple, as a forestay and two main shrouds over crosstrees are all that is needed to support it. The mainsail and headsail are so small that they can easily be sheeted and handled; there is a spinnaker for off the wind sailing, so the crew is of equal importance to the helmsman, which makes this an ideal boat in which to learn the art of sailing. With its detachable keel the boat can be put on top of a small car and the keel in the boot, or she can be taken home and stored on a rack for winter, for the rudder is portable as well as the keel.

As well as affording exciting yet safe high-speed sailing, this Flying Family has rules insisting on buoyant apparatus, so that even when swamped and full of water they will float their crew, hull, keel and all gear—a safety precaution which applies to very few keel-class boats.

There are many other wonderful little keel boats. For two adults the Flying Fifteen at £350 is most suitable, and for three adults the X Class One-Design at £850. This X Class was designed for the Royal Motor Yacht Club by Alfred Westmacot, M.R.I.N.A., of Woodnuts at Bembridge, and these little day racers have had a triumphant forty-year career.

Because of their quiet modesty they have only spread from Bembridge, Hythe, Hamble, and through the Solent from Poole to Chichester, almost as if the people sailing them wished to keep the secret of their ability from the rest of the world. There are about 120 of them in existence, and as many as 50 of these race during Cowes Week.

As they have no planing ability, it is senseless to pile on sail area in blowing weather to a dangerous extent in the hope of lifting the boat up and scooting over the top of the water. So you will always find the Xs reefed to suit the weather and will seldom see them in difficulties.

Length Overall: 20′ 9″ (6·230m)	*Length Waterline:* 17′ (5·181m)
Beam: 6′ (1·828m)	*Draught:* 3′ (·914m)
Displacement: 1 *ton* (1,016 *kilos*)	*Sail Area:* 186 *sq. ft.* (17·28 *sq. m*)

These dimensions tell of a sound, sensible, sturdy and seaman-like little vessel, and a study of the plans reveals that the keel is almost half the waterline length which makes the vessel steady on her helm and easy for grounding or putting on a slipway for scraping and painting. The straight top and bottom of the iron ballast keel, which weighs 12½ cwt., makes for simplicity not only in the moulding of the keel but also in the framework of the main keel. Her two sling bolts through the main keel at either end of the iron ballast keel enable her to be lifted out of the water or put on a slipway at will by the owner.

The table of scantlings calls for a sturdy little vessel as the planking must be ⅝ in. thick and the rest of her scantlings are matched to this sturdiness. Her open cockpit is so large that it can take half a dozen people, which makes her an ideal boat for day sailing, picnicking as well as racing.

From her lines we note that all the waterlines are fairly parallel to each other, that the buttocks are sweeping and easy, while her firm bilge gives her power to carry sail and is so well shaped that it is difficult to put your finger on the turn of the bilge. Studying these plans with an understanding eye, we can discover why for forty years these boats have been so popular with so many people with knowledge of the sea and its ways (see page 44).

When she was designed the Bermudian rig had not arrived, so when I used to enjoy racing with the late Harry Brickwood we had a great deal of fun changing the shape of the mainsail. For with a gaff you have a four-sided sail which you can play about with, altering its shape by peaking it high or dropping the gaff. So, though the Bermudian rig is more efficient than the old gaff, it has taken some of the fun and skill out of sailing. All you can do now is to set your sail. There is nothing to play about with, whereas with

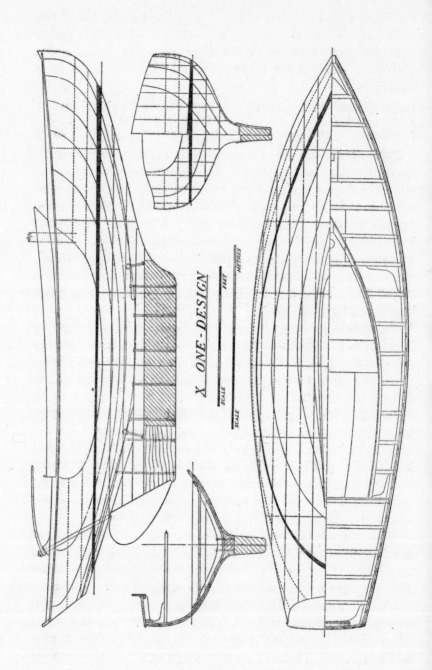

X ONE - DESIGN

SCALE ___ FEET

SCALE ___ METRES

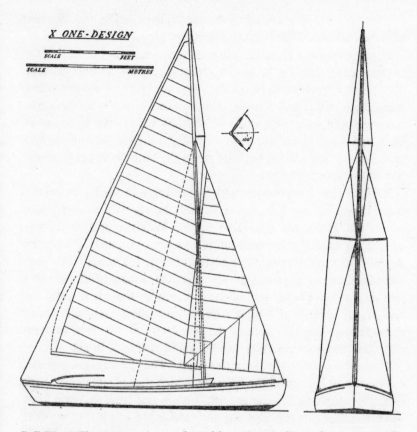

Sail Plan: The runner shown dotted is optional. Since the mast stands quite well without it, it is seldom fitted, so that in tacking only the jib sheet has to be tended.

(*Left*) **Lines:** These lines show the long parallel iron keel which adds strength to the vessel; the sections show a wide and stable bilge, making for seaworthiness and comfort; the lower part of the plan shows the 8-ft. cockpit in which six people can sail comfortably.

the old four-sided mainsail there was endless fun in the different adjustments you could make in different strengths of wind.

I well remember Harry Brickwood insisting on an overall cover to the cockpit of his X boats, for although people do not realise it, the sun shining down through the open cockpit can disturb paint, roughing it with small blisters, although this is on the underside of the vessel and under water. So we see that racing used to be just as keen and hard in the old days as today, and the helmsman who took the greatest care of his boat stood the best chance of winning, just as he does today.

The sail plan has gone through two changes in the history of the class. Some thirty years ago a Bermudian rig with a long main-boom was fitted, but after the 1939–45 War the present rig was adopted, and as the mainsail luff is now approximately double the length of the mainboom it is a perfect rig for this vessel. The top-mast backstay, going from the stern to the topmast head, with two jumper stays, takes the pull of the forestay, so there is no need for runners to support this mast fore and aft. The main and lower shrouds each side take care of the side loads, so we often see men and their wives successfully handling and racing X boats.

There is an unusual rule in this class. The flat spinnaker is not allowed to be set round the forestay, which makes spinnaker work simpler, easier and less dangerous. I hope and trust they will keep this spinnaker rule and also that they will bring in a rule to say that no one may sit out over the side of these vessels or upon the deck, as the older I grow the more I admire the X boat and want in a few years' time to go back to racing in them as I did when I was fairly young.

Then there are the Victory One-Design classes, modelled on the old Bembridge One-Designs—seaworthy little vessels, clinker built, suitable for two adults—at £650.

All these five boats will teach you to sail and will give you the freedom and peace only to be found on the sea.

After a season or so spent learning to sail in a non-capsizing boat, the younger generation should go into the drop-keel craft, and here again there are hundreds to choose from. We are now about to embark in a boat where a mistake or any slowness of thought or action can cause a capsize, with all hands overboard and the mast and sail in the sea, so that our boat looks like an exhausted bird on the waves. Whatever boat we choose, it should have buoyant chambers, capable of floating hull and crew. Fortunately, most drop-keel classes not only have buoyant rules for the boat, but also insist that all aboard should wear buoyant garments.

For two children the International Cadet, 10 ft. 5 in. overall at £85, is the boat. Its simplicity of shape enables it to be built by amateurs at home from a kit set for as little as £48, and in this they can continue to sail until they are sixteen years of age. Then they can go into the 12-ft. Firefly, a National One-Design, faster and livelier, at £130—or £85, if built from a kit-set at home. Because of its ability, a Firefly is also a good boat for two lightweight adults, weighing 22 stone between them (a man and wife, perhaps).

The size of boat for two men of normal weight is 14 ft., and we have many one-designs of this size. There is the hard-chine *Yachting World* General Purpose 14-footer at £165—or £120, if built from a kit-set at home. This is a sturdy, fairly safe boat, not exciting or calling for great skill, for as her name implies she is a general purpose boat.

For the seas that sweep in from the Atlantic on the coasts of Devon and Cornwall, there is the 14-ft. Redwing, a speedy yet powerful boat because of her generous sail area and fast lines. Unlike most drop-keel classes that have sacrificed seaworthiness for speed by fitting wooden drop-keels, the Redwing must sail with a galvanised drop-keel weighing 125 lb. which, with her powerful form, gives her great steadiness in a breeze of wind with a sea running.

For three people there is the 18-ft. Jolly Boat, very fast, exciting and fairly free from capsizing, as its drop-keel is of galvanised steel; though it weighs only 65 lb., when she is knocked over to an angle of 45° by a squall its tendency is to sink and right her—whereas at this angle a wooden drop-keel tends to float to the surface and so has a capsizing influence. The Jolly Boat costs £300—or £220, if built from a kit-set at home.

Once we have learnt the basic technique of sailing, we can go on to a boat where we also need the ability and agility of a tight-rope walker—to a Dutchman, a 5.0.5 or an International 10-metre

Canoe. The Dutchman is 20 ft. overall and is sailed by only two men, who must be strong and powerful. Even so, the crew has a wire to windward from the hounds and a body-belt so that with the wire clipped on he stands full-length out from the side of the boat, and his weight to windward enables a boat that should have a crew of four to be sailed by only two.

The 5.0.5 is 16 ft. 6 in. long and is really a three-man boat, but the crew suspended to windward by a wire from the mast at jib halyard height enables this boat to be sailed by only two as well. Both these classes call for the highest degree of skill in the helmsman and crew, who must be athletes, acrobats and, in addition, highly skilled seamen. Both the Dutchman and the 5.0.5 cost £350.

Finally there is the International 10-metre Canoe, costing £350. Here there is only one man, and he must be a perfectionist in sailing, balance and acrobatics. Here, too, we have come out of the regimentation of a one-design class and are free to design and build whatever shape we desire within the class restrictions, so that as well as progressing in sailing skill we may also progress in the design and construction of the vessel itself. We have arrived at the top, the high-water-mark of sailing drop-keel craft. The peak of perfection in sailing is found in this canoe, "the dry fly of sailing". Here we have the fastest boat of its size in the world, a light, sensitive thoroughbred only kept on its feet by the extreme skill and agility of its single-handed sailor who is at one and the same time her complete crew and helmsman.

When putting his canoe through the wind on to the other tack, he lets fly the jibsheet, flattens his mainsail, puts his helm down, eases himself in off the end of the sliding-seat and brings this inboard as the wind pressure is reduced on his sails. Then he moves his weight across the centre-line as the canoe bow swings across the wind, pushes his sliding-seat out on the new weather side, trims his jib and secures it, straightens up his tiller, moves himself out to the end of his sliding-seat which extends five feet beyond the weather side of his canoe, adjusting his mainsheet as he goes. All this in a matter of ten seconds. Now away he goes, swifter than any other craft, flying low over the water on the end of his sliding seat.

The Flying Twenty-Five *Kingfisher* planing at 16 knots over an empty Solent when the Regatta was postponed because of a gale. Like the Flying Twelve, this boat is designed to plane over the surface of the water and can therefore be driven really hard in a strong wind.

Britannia winning her 200th race, travelling at her maximum speed of 13¼ knots, with her crew on the weather deck to keep her upright. Unlike *Kingfisher*, she is a displacement vessel without planing ability, so she cannot be driven any faster than this, so rightly has a two-reefed mainsail.

X Class boats running before a strong breeze that has whipped the sea into a silvery foam. The spinnakers are set inside the forestay, since the class rule does not allow them to be set round it as is usual today.

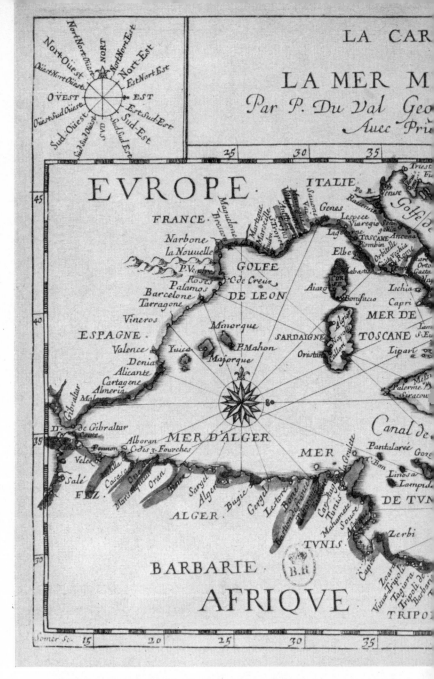

This French chart, dated 1630, shows how the old names for compass points were derived from the Italian words for the winds of the Mediterranean (*see diagram at top right*). Then came the French words (*see diagram at top left*), which are like our own—though you can still make

out the Fleur-de-Lis and the Cross marking North and East, because in the Mediterranean France is to the North and Jerusalem is to the East. Today, all the colour is going out of life so we just have numbers of degrees—ah, me!

The 10-Metre Canoe planing along at top speed. The helmsman must watch the water to windward for squalls and not be caught napping, or else he will come to grief . . .

... as I have here. I haul the boat up against the wind ...

... until I am able to get one leg over the side ...

. . . and am
soon off on
course again.

Avenger winning the Prince of Wales' Cup in 1928. This historic picture (reproduced from an old photograph) shows her at top speed with the mainsail eased away in a squall so that only a few feet of the clew are drawing; a full mainsail would capsize her (see pages 66 and 74).

I've sailed in every kind of craft—square-rigged vessels, the lordly "J" Class, 23-metres, 19-metres, 15-metres, 12- 8- 6·50- 6- 5·5- and 5-metres; catamarans and cruisers, and exciting centre-board craft—but no boat on this earth compares with the "dry fly of sailing" for exhilaration and the pure delight of sailing. In this canoe the least error brings about the tragedy of a capsize and exquisite skill takes her along at an ever-increasing and exciting speed.

Not many aspire to this state of sailing perfection. In the British Isles there is the Royal Clyde Canoe Club, with only twenty active canoeists sailing on the loveliness of Loch Lomond; the Humber Yawl Club now sailing cruising canoe yawls, with only three sliding-seat canoe enthusiasts; and the Royal Canoe Club with its headquarters on Trowlock Island on the Thames, and its twenty-five active sliding-seat canoeists who sail on the south coast at Hayling Island. In America, the New York Canoe Club has thirty active members sailing on Long Island Sound and Sugar Island, one of the thousand islands on the border of U.S.A. and Canada. In Sweden, there are twenty-four canoe sailors. So while there are thousands upon thousands sailing the easily handled drop-keel boats, only one hundred in the whole world can aspire to such perfection as the International sliding-seat canoe demands of its owners. Yet a sliding-seat canoe, perfection in the builder's art, costs only £350 to build.

We could range through a great variety of small, drop-keel craft in which to finish our apprenticeship to the sea. All have their virtues and flaws. The light drop-keel craft, being easily transported and drawing little water, have the advantage of giving their owners the choice of a wide variety of sailing waters, sea and inland, and they can easily be trailed behind or carried on top of a motor-car.

A man or woman starting to sail at forty years of age or over would do well to learn with the steadiness and security of keel craft, and to remain constant to them. In these they will find peace and joy as well as many an exciting sail, for the sea is forever changing its mood from storm to sunshine and from calm to gale, and with a keel boat we can enjoy all these moods.

There is a greater range and variety of ballast-keel boats than of drop-keel boats, for they are sometimes great, stable ships.

D

There are vessels which have drop-keels running down through their ballast keels—a bastard breed—and while these have the advantages of both types they also have the disadvantages of both, for you cannot get a half-crown for sixpence in this world. Several of this breed have disappeared at sea through those on board believing they had the qualities of a keel boat when this is only partly true. For where shallow, flat-floored hulls have great initial stability, once they are hove down beyond a certain angle of heel this disappears and where a normal keel boat has the righting power of her ballast keel low down—usually half her total weight these days—the shallow draft boat lacks this great safety factor. Because they are larger and involve more labour and materials, keel boats increase enormously in price with size.

We enter this world with nothing but two instincts, one to survive and the other to procreate ourselves; we go to school, start work and not until we arrive at the roaring forties can we hope to have any control or money. This is of no great importance for all the best things in life are free, the sea, the sky, and the countryside. When young we are lusty enough to be needed by the over-forties to trim the sails of their boats, to help with their horses, guns, dogs and fishing gear; then when we arrive at this splendid age we, too, can have our larger vessels and take out youngsters to help us enjoy them. So at forty, when we need the greater security and comfort of keel boats, we can have them. There is an infinite variety but generally they fall into four groups: day sailing, day racing, cruising, and ocean racing.

The day sailer needs all the qualities of a day racer. We are only going to sail a few hours so we need a sparkling, lively vessel, swift and yet safe. The International Dragon at £1,500, or the International One-Design at £2,500, are sensible ships for day sailing and racing, as well as those of a lesser price suitable for the beginners. All these have qualities that only the expert can bring out.

Then there are the International Yacht Racing Union Classes 6-, 8-, 10-, 12-metres, ranging in price from £3,000 to £30,000. While they are all built to Lloyd's scantling and survey they are not one-designs, every designer and owner striving to get the utmost out of the formulae, the answer to which must be 6 or 12-metres, or whatever the metric class she is to race in. This rule has been in force for fifty years, with modifications, and produces powerful, seaworthy vessels with terrific drive to windward. On this point of sailing no other type of boat can compare with them for, as well as being shapely, they have three-quarters of their weight in their lead ballast keels low down. In 1954, the I.Y.R.U. decided to abandon the 6-metre Class but in 1959, just five years after, no less than four new 6-metres were being built in Europe. The America's Cup is now raced for in 12-metres and it is probable that this will increase the interest in these wonderful racers. A Six is exactly half a Twelve, while an Eight, being closer to the Twelve and having cabin accommodation, will give owners an indication of the ability of their design, the formulae being exactly alike for all, the only difference being in the scantlings for hull and masts.

Books on sailing have been written by men with very limited knowledge who have never designed, built or raced and have only cruised a little. But they have a boundless love of the sea and such a great belief in themselves that they claim to speak the Word of God, whereas all they really do is to rewrite the false doctrine written by earlier men, also writing without full knowledge of their subject. Men like this believe the earth to be flat, the "Flat Earthists". There can be but very few of these left today; any man can now write of the moon but in a few years the only ones qualified will be those who return from that planet. These egoists who write of boats they have never known of do harm because they mislead people.

They say that the International Yacht Racing Union Metre Racing Classes (i) are unseaworthy; (ii) are difficult to steer; (iii) are bad in a seaway as all their ballast is in the form of an outside keel; (iv) will not heave-to; (v) have a weak construction. Every one of these statements is false, and the last is a libel on Lloyd's, as these classes are all built to Lloyd's scantlings and survey. I have made long passages in these metre boats and often hove-to in them. If they were difficult to steer they would never win races. The fact that they are owned by the foremost yachtsmen in countries all over the world, are from the boards of the leading designers, and built to the standards of Lloyds, whose knowledge of construction is unrivalled and whose honesty of purpose has been recognised for 200 years, should make such writers reflect.

Unfortunately, it does not, and we have to endure a lot of misery (where two or three yachtsmen are gathered together) listening to utter nonsense.

A new class, the $5\frac{1}{2}$-metre, was formed to replace the Sixes under another formula, but they have not enough sail area to make them interesting to sail in light weather, neither have they enough power nor are they manly enough to give enjoyment in a breeze. All of which explains why, although declared dead by the I.Y.R.U., the Six Metres still flourish.

Then there are cruiser vessels that are floating homes. A quarter of a century ago I wrote that the "best ocean racer is the best cruiser". Ocean-going yachts racing across the Atlantic, Pacific or from an Australian port or round the Fastnet, will encounter every kind of weather from calm and light airs to heavy gales. Those on board must be kept in perfect health to race their ship hard for twenty-four hours of every day of the weeks or months they are at sea. The vessels and their gear must be perfect to endure being driven to the utmost, as they must be to win, so it naturally follows that a good ocean racer is a good cruiser.

With an able vessel under him, a man can choose whether to drive along fast or jill along at a comfortable clip, for it is by the number of seas we ride over or crash through a minute that we measure our comfort. The man with a slower boat has no choice; he can only go slow and in all probability half his ballast is inside, a messy and dangerous arrangement brought about by his boat being evolved and not properly designed. The owner of a cruiser must beware of unseamanlike lines by inferior designers who, unable to design normal, fairly fleet and seaworthy craft, seek for and discover flaws in the Ocean Racing Club Rule and design to suit the weakness of the rule and not the might and strength of the sea. Any ship that seeks a living at sea is given a good sheer line and the bow is high to ride over the oncoming seas, for her speed increases the speed of their approach. The Yacht Racing Association and the I.Y.R.U. rules call for "the sheer to be a continuous concave curve", but the Royal Ocean Racing Club, a much newer body, was not wise enough to insist on this law proved by the sea. The R.O.R.C. measured length is between a girth station each end, so some designers prostituted their art and drew vessels intended for the sea with a hogged back sheer, as this reduced the bow and stern girth measurement, and so reduced the measured length and rating by the Rule, thus giving a good handicap.

Sea-going ships of all nations throughout the ages—Viking ships, giant oil tankers, fishing vessels, lifeboats—all have a good sheer for the sea. We read in the Bible that Saint Paul "cast four anchors out of the stern and wished for the day". The stern of his ship was highest and so best able to ride over the seas. So look for a good cruiser amongst the ocean racers, but beware of the misshapen, hump-backed, pregnant prawns.

A man should have a vessel equal in length to his age. At ten years a 10-ft. dinghy will be within the strength and understanding of two boys. At twenty, two young men can happily endure the discomfort of cruising in an International Dragon (at least they could and did before the racing element in the class destroyed the cabin top and the idea of week-end cruising on which this class was built up). At seventy, a man can be looked after by skipper, crew and steward on a 70-footer. There is a vessel for every kind of sailing in every clime, every purpose and age; all we have to do is to set out our requirements clearly and then we can find a vessel to "our heart's delight" that will sail us happily over the seas we choose.

It is easier to learn by day sailing and to perfect our sailing technique by day racing in which every mistake and clumsy movement can be measured in seconds, minutes and boat's lengths lost. This chapter deals only with day boats; cruisers, in which you live aboard, explore new lands and cook aboard, are dealt with in a later chapter.

III

How To Sail

ABOVE all else, we must remember that wind is power. It has driven windmills to grind corn into flour and pumped water throughout the ages. This power can be measured, as the following table will show. Seamen in the past put the wind's strength into twelve groups, but never stated its actual speed or power. All these are here set side by side with the original scale devised by Admiral Beaufort, and the graph illustrates the wind pressures at the various speeds between those on the scale.

We must learn to judge the wind speed and, from this, gauge its pressure by its effect on the water when at sea and its effect on trees when we are ashore. Then, by constant study we learn what its power is and how it is likely to develop, so that we are never caught by surprise.

BEAUFORT SCALE AND EQUIVALENTS

Beaufort Scale	Definition	Wind Speed (m.p.h.)	Wind Pressure (lb. per sq. ft.)	Wave Height (ft. approx.)
0	Calm	0	0	0
1	Light air	2	·01	0
2	Light breeze	5	·08	½
3	Gentle breeze	9	·28	2
4	Moderate breeze	13	·67	3½
5	Fresh breeze	19	1·31	6
6	Strong breeze	24	2·3	9½
7	Moderate gale	30	3·6	13½
8	Fresh gale	37	5·4	18
9	Strong gale	44	7·7	23
10	Whole gale	51	10·5	29
11	Storm	60	14·0	37
12	Hurricane	65+	17·0+	45+

A thoughtful study of the last table will be of great assistance
to our sailing, as it tells us that the pressure in pounds per square
foot is doubled from 19 to 26 m.p.h., so that broadly speaking as
19 m.p.h. is the speed of wind in which we would think of reefing
for comfort in a cruising boat at sea when beating to windward,
we should reef to approximately half her sail area in a wind of
26 m.p.h. We do not do this, however, as today we reef our
sails at the foot, thus lowering the pressure and so increasing the
amount of sail we can carry. So we reef only a third not a half.

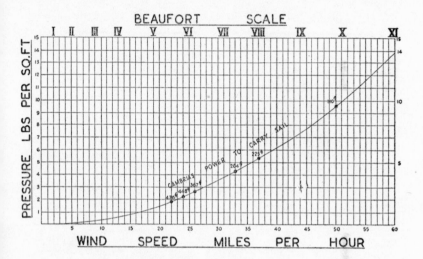

There are several things to realise about the power of wind and
its pressure; if it is blowing 20 m.p.h. we increase this to 26 m.p.h.
when we are driving our vessel to windward at a speed of six
knots, but if we are chasing away before the same wind at eight
knots, we reduce the wind's speed felt by our ship to 12 m.p.h.
and its pressure is reduced to one half, which explains why we
can and do set the enormous spinnakers off the wind. Then, too,
tidal currents affect the wind. In the same 20 m.p.h. wind a 4-knot
tide making against the wind will increase the apparent wind to
24 m.p.h., while the same strength tide running with the wind will
decrease the wind felt by a vessel to 16 m.p.h.—points to be borne
in mind when deciding which and what sail to set and whether to
reef or not.

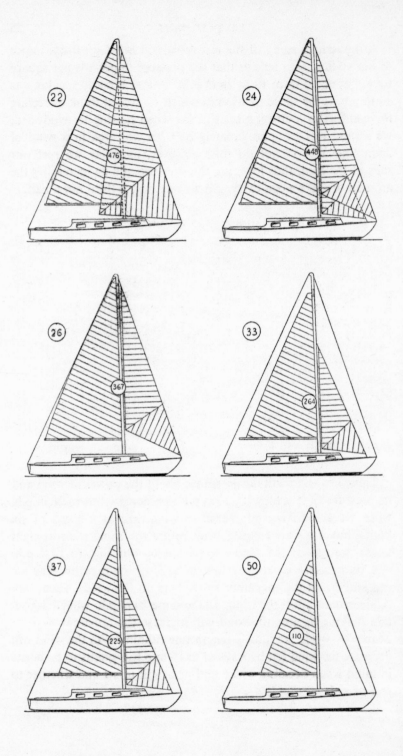

There is yet another thing to remember: the wind is never true in strength or direction, and if you listen to weather reports you will often hear the announcer say "Wind south-west 20 m.p.h., gusting up to 25 m.p.h." The westerlies, however, are truer than the easterlies; these can and do swing to and fro 2 and 3 points— even the steady North-East Trades in Latitudes 18° to 28° vary greatly—so we must remember that an easterly is never true anywhere in the world.

When cruising, we reef and adjust our sail area to suit the squalls and when racing to suit the lulls, so a cruiser is comfortable in the gusts and undercanvassed in between them, whereas the racer is overpowered and struggling in the squalls. In these the mainsheet should be eased in the smaller vessels and the larger ships sailed just a little finer to ease the pressure and keep them on their feet so they can continue at top speed. All vessels large or small sail slower when heeled, so we must never confuse blustering fuss with speed and ability. Now study the six sail plans of the 24-ft. waterline cruiser, and you will see the reduction in sail area in winds from 22 to 50 m.p.h. required to keep constant the total pressure the vessel can stand. The circle to the left gives the winds speed in m.p.h. and the sail area and the position of the centre of pressure is shown in the middle of the sail set.

Now while sails in the ends of a boat enable us to control and twist her about, the nearer they are to the centre the better they drive her and here they can be handled more safely and easily as they are not only in the centre of the see-saw where the motion is less but here the boat is wider with more room to work. So as the gale increases take in all sails possible at the ends of the vessel and drive her from amidships. Then if, finally, you must take in all sail because the gale has increased beyond what your

(*Left*) Six *Cambria* Sail Plans: These plans show *Cambria's* change of sail in various winds. The masthead rig sets the maximum sail on a given length of mast, but puts a great strain on the masthead itself. In stronger winds it is best to set a staysail on the lower stay, both to spread the strain and to make the work o the crew easier by splitting the headsail area in two.

canvas, spars or vessel can stand, your final operation is carried out in the comparative safety of 'midships.

The graph (page 55) gives the wind speeds and corresponding pressures. A deep keel vessel is stable even when she is hove down to an angle of 120° heel. She could, therefore, be considered self-righting for all practical purposes, for once her wooden spars are underwater they float and the sea that would be running in wind enough to put her down to such an angle would also strike her upright in the twinkling of an eye.

This is true also of any well-designed deep-keeled vessel with approximately half its weight in its outside ballast keel, for if knocked down by a sea, provided hatches are closed and no water gets below, she will right herself with the next sea, just as *Typhoon*, a ketch, did when three friends and myself were sailing her across the Atlantic. Almost all drop-keel craft would, however, remain capsized, because their ballast keels are not low enough to give a righting factor.

We cannot sail directly into the wind but, as the diagram on the opposite page shows, we can sail within approximately 45° of it. Some boats can sail closer than this, others are not so close-winded, so it is sensible and seamanlike to assume that your boat will sail at 45° to the wind. Then if you discover she can sail closer you are delighted, and if she is not so close-winded you are less disappointed.

The art of sailing is to find out exactly what your boat will and will not do, and to quietly encourage her to do her utmost with the least interference from you and the least possible use of the rudder. The rudder steers and controls the vessel but in doing so it acts as a brake and reduces speed; so we see the best helmsman is the one who allows the boat to sail with the least use of the rudder.

To sail close-hauled, at an angle of 45° to the wind, we flatten in all the sails until they are as close to the centre line as our vessel will bear, adjusting all the sails (marrying them together), so that all lift and shake at once. If we have one sail flatter than another, it presses the boat unduly and tends to heel the boat over rather than drive her ahead in perfect unison with the others. Now our sails are adjusted to a nicety we must sail our vessel as close to the wind as we can, yet still keep her footing fast.

POINTS OF SAILING

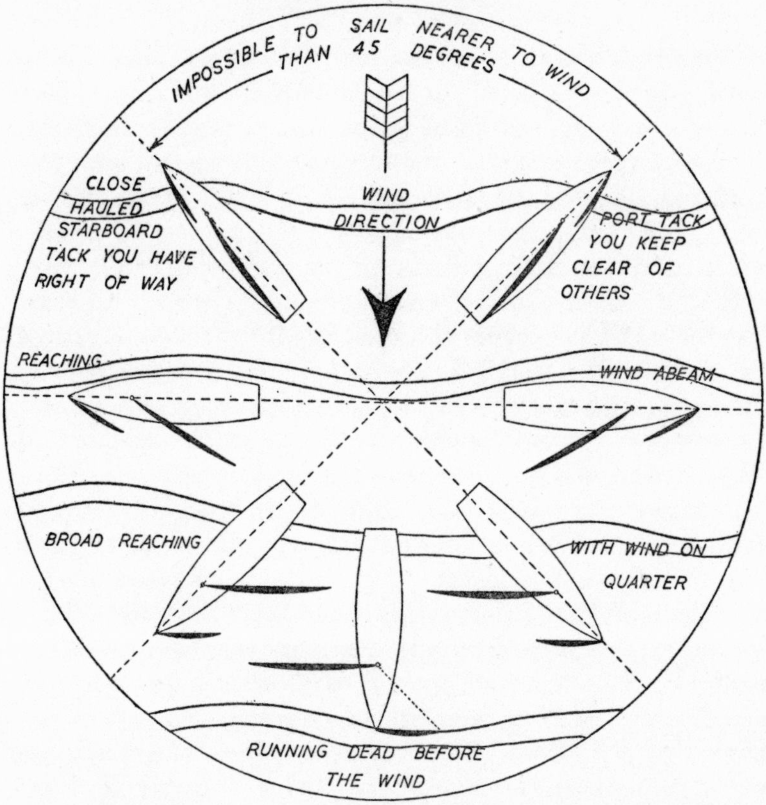

IMPOSSIBLE TO SAIL NEARER THAN 45 DEGREES TO WIND

WIND
DIRECTION

CLOSE
HAULED
STARBOARD
TACK YOU HAVE
RIGHT OF WAY

PORT TACK
YOU KEEP
CLEAR OF
OTHERS

REACHING

WIND ABEAM

BROAD REACHING

WITH WIND ON
QUARTER

RUNNING DEAD BEFORE
THE WIND

Broadly speaking, if we have flattened our sails down hard we must sail her with a good rap full, but if the sails are not hardened down we need not fill them so hard. To sail directly into the wind's eye we sail first on one tack 45° to the wind, then we go through the wind on the other tack at a right angle (90°) to our old course and battle our boat to windward on a zigzag course—always at a 45° angle to the wind like a drunken man, only accurately.

The easiest and fastest point of sailing is reaching with the wind abeam (90° from the centre-line of our vessel). Here we sail exactly where we wish to go, and once on course the sails should be eased off until they shake and lift, then hauled in just enough to send them to sleep when they drive us to their utmost on our course.

Broad reaching is almost as easy a point of sailing, but now the wind is well abaft the beam (135° to the centre-line of our vessel over her quarter). Once more, when on course the sails are eased to the utmost as, the farther off the sails are, the less they press and heel the boat and the more they drive her ahead. But here the steering is more difficult, for where with a beam wind the seas strike the vessel squarely all along her sides and have little effect on her course, they now lift her stern and in lifting her take away from her length supported by the water. This lessens her power to carry sail, causing her to heel to leeward and to dig in her bows, all of which makes her surge to windward in a wild swoop and so makes it difficult to steer a straight and true course. The good helmsman watches each wave, judges unconsciously the effect this is going to have and, quite naturally and without thought, firmly gives her just the right amount of helm to counteract it. He anticipates every movement of the vessel and, by applying rudder before his ship starts to root, uses the minimum of helm.

Running, your vessel is dead before the wind, which is 180° from the centre-line right over your tail, and this is the most dangerous and difficult point of sailing. If you allow your vessel to swing enough to take the wind across her stern more than one point—$11\frac{1}{4}$° —it will get behind the mainsail and whoop! bang! the mainsail and mainboom fly across from one side to the other with terrific speed and power. In a brisk breeze the boom could kill a man or carry away rigging and bring down the mast. Then your proud ship would be like a sea-bird with a broken wing, at the mercy of wind and wave. Therefore when running in blowing weather, the steersman must be forever watchful.

With all this in mind, we can now start to sail with complete understanding. To make it easy for our first lesson we will sail in a wind of 15 m.p.h., a moderate breeze, with the wind abeam at an angle of 90° to the centre-line—the natural point of sailing to start on. You steer a steady course, straight across the wind towards a point on the land, a cloud in the distant sky, a star, or by your compass. If you are steering by compass, watch the sky ahead as well as the point or quarter-point you are steering on the compass. This not only rests your eye, but enables you to steer a truer course, for you see your bow swinging against the sky much more quickly than the alteration of the comparatively small compass card, and the card itself even in a liquid compass swings a little.

Now you ease the headsail until it shakes on the luff and haul it back until its luff ceases to tremble. Once the jib is sheeted correctly you ease out the main and treat this in the same manner. From time to time ease the jibsheet till the headsail shakes, then haul in until it ceases to tremble. Any time you can leave it out without having to sheet in all you have eased out you will find that the wind has freed you and you can then let out the mainsail this amount, remembering that the more your sails are off the centre-line the more they push you ahead.

During the last thirty years a great many people have in their writings proved that a sail works in exactly the same way as an aeroplane wing, and that all the power developed is on the lee of the sail, which is the equivalent to the top surface of the aeroplane's wing. My belief, however, is that sails are deflectors: that they turn the wind backward towards the stern and that the reaction pushes the vessel forward. If, as some theorists maintain, they have the lift on their lee side, corresponding to the upper-surface of an aeroplane's wing, then this force is taking the boat to leeward; so the only time it acts ahead is when the sails are squared right across the centre-line of your vessel.

Whatever you think, at all times struggle, struggle, struggle to square your sails off the fore and aft line of your ship, for the more square the sails the more they push you ahead, and the more upright your vessel is the easier and faster she will sail.

The Royal Aeronautical Establishment at Farnborough, our greatest air experts, have proved conclusively that a bee, light or laden, cannot fly. Unfortunately they have not, through all the years they have known this, found the means to impart this important information to the bee who, in his ignorance, happily continues to fly heavy-laden with nectar for honey. So we, too, should continue to sail happily without destroying the pure magic of swishing silently through the sea by too much doubtful theory.

If you steer with a wheel you turn the wheel naturally the way you wish the ship's head to turn. If, however, as is more probable when you are learning (as you should) in a small craft, you are steering with a tiller, then you pull or push the tiller the opposite way to that in which you wish your ship's head to turn. This is because the tiller, or bar as the French so aptly call it, is fixed to the rudder-head and when you put the tiller to port you put the rudder-blade to starboard, which swings the stern to port and the bow to starboard, and vice versa. The more you use the rudder the slower you will sail, as first of all the rudder across your stern acts as a brake and, secondly, you will be sailing an erratic and therefore a longer course. So as you learn to sail on this, the easiest point of sailing, be firm but as quiet as you can with the helm.

With the wind square abeam the seas, large or small, will also be coming exactly abeam, parallel to your fore and aft centre-line. So your vessel will rise boldly and equally fore and aft, showing no tendency to swerve off course, another reason why this is the easiest point of sailing. You can reach to and fro easily and safely for an hour, by which time you will be settled and at home at the helm. As you put your vessel through the wind to take her from one tack to the other, spring her round by hauling in on the mainsheet as you put your helm down. Then the sail will continue to drive your boat until she is head to wind, when you should ease away the amount of the mainsheet you have hauled in to spring her into wind and allow her to fall off on the new tack until she is once more sailing at an angle of 90° to the wind.

The jib can be kept sheeted while the bow is swinging into wind because, though in the normal way you would now be spilling the wind from it because the bow is springing fast and scooping wind, this sail will continue to pull a few more seconds. When it shakes, you ease away on the sheet and haul in on the new lee jibsheet, trimming the jib correctly on the new tack. Reaching to and fro for one hour will teach you how to steer, how to trim your sheets and how to go through the wind on to the other tack.

When going about the steersman should call in a commanding yet questioning voice "Ready about!"—then, when the crew have confirmed their understanding and readiness by repeating "Ready about!", the steersman calls "Lee-ho!" as he puts the helm down or a-lee.

Broad reaching means sailing farther away from the wind, and after half an hour of sailing on a broad reach you will have added to your steering ability. Now you are sailing with the wind on your quarter, 135° away from the wind, still a safe but not quite such an easy course to steer. You are three-quarters away from the wind and as the waves travel dead before it and range square across the wind, they first of all lift your weather quarter and depress your lee bow, upsetting the fore and aft balance of your boat. She will immediately try to shoot into the wind, and this you must firmly stop by a quick pull to windward on the tiller. Now the wave lifts the bow, the stern sinks, and your vessel sheers to leeward; again you must apply firm helm quickly in the opposite direction. If you wait a fraction of a second too long your vessel starts broaching into wind or sheering away from it and then a great deal of helm must be applied. The good helmsman watches every wave and, judging its effect on his ship, applies helm just before she starts off course. By anticipating the sheer he saves a great deal of fierce steering. The stronger the wind the greater the seas, and only tip-top steersmen can cope when a vessel is being driven to the utmost under such conditions.

Some twenty-five years ago, we were racing up-Channel before a gale of wind with full mainsail and a large spinnaker set. We could drive like this as our vessel, usually manned by four, had eight able men aboard, which gave us the power and ability to smother our sails quickly in any weight of wind. The wind and sea increased until finally although all eight were first-rate men, only three of us were competent enough to steer. And though we usually steered for four or more hours we could now only take the wheel for 45 to 60 minutes at a time. We had to watch every sea, anticipate our boat's every movement—whether she would suddenly want to broach, or run off and gybe—and counteract each move with a quick turn of the wheel before it started. If we had left it too late and she had started to broach, our control would have been lost. With darkness the wind, as so often happens, eased, and others were then able to steer. So, though broad reaching is next to the easiest point of sailing, driving hard before a quartering wind and sea can demand our utmost.

Until now, we have only used our jib and mainsail, so sail handling and steering have been as simple as possible. Now we shall set a spinnaker and chase away dead before the wind. Once the spinnaker is set it demands the utmost from the steersman, who cannot for a moment take his eye off its luff, or outer edge, as this enormous sail, often twice the area of the mainsail, is set flying by its halyard and held captive only here and at its two lower corners by the sheet and guy. Ballooning away from these three points of attachment, it can collapse as swift as light, so from the moment it is decided that the spinnaker be set until it is safely stowed, constant vigilance is required.

In days gone by the spinnaker was set only when chasing away dead before the wind, but now it is set with the wind from right aft to abeam, as different racing classes have limitations on their jibs and can only increase their sail area by setting their spinnakers which are sometimes three times the area of mainsail. These great sails, with little limitations, are set by racers with advantage on all possible and sometimes impossible occasions.

It is to this practice that we owe our present-day knowledge of spinnaker shapes and the art of setting and handling them. Now you are steering more before the wind so that it is fine over the stern to starboard, at the same time easing off the mainsail until the sail aloft is square across the ship. Many men with years of sailing experience ease away their mainsails beyond this point, without ever realising that this is an uncomfortable thing to do, and dangerous to centreboard craft, as it has caused more to capsize than any other flaw in sail setting and handling.

Once the mainsheet has been eased away so much that some of the mainsail aloft is forward of the mast, a weather roll is instantly set up, as the wind pressure so high up has a telling effect, and the power of it on the mainsail forward of the mast rolls the boat to windward. Now her weather bilge is submerged and its power, plus the waves on the weather side, rolls the boat to leeward. So rhythmic rolling is set up. Cruising men endure this for days, and small racing centreboards capsize—all because they do not know that to allow any part of the mainsail forward of the mast is uncomfortable and dangerous.

Years ago when we were chasing away across the Atlantic from Madeira to the Bermudas in the 20-ton schooner *Diablesse* before the strong North-East Trades, we rolled with our square sails set, so we hoisted and set our mainsail and kept it sheeted fairly flat although on a dead run. The gaff laid off fairly square, but the boom was fairly well in. This gave us more drive with safety and the vast area, practically fore and aft, low down in the mainsail damped out the rolling; so life on board was again comfortable.

Points to Remember

(1) Boats can carry all the sail they can set in winds up to 20 m.p.h.

(2) Boats that only go in a breeze over 20 m.p.h. are undercanvassed, as all should go at a good clip in a 12-m.p.h. breeze; while those that are overpowered in winds below 20 m.p.h. are overcanvassed.

(3) Winds are never true in strength or direction. When racing, you reef so that you are seamanlike in the lulls and smothered in the squalls; when cruising you reef so that you are comfortable in the squalls and undercanvassed in the lulls.

(4) Displacement boats can sail only at the square root of waterline length close-hauled, and half as fast again in perfect speed conditions reaching across the wind. These are their maximum speeds, and once these speeds are reached and maintained these vessels should reef, whether racing or cruising, as carrying sail beyond this is unseamanlike and only leads to strains.

(5) A graph showing the sail area of *Cambria*, a 24-footer, being reduced as wind speeds and pressure mount explains all this at a glance on page 55. The fact that the wind pressures are reduced as the wind speed increases, because all the water surface several feet deep is sliding to leeward, has not been allowed for, as now the seas are so great that often the vessel is only half-supported momentarily as the seas race by her.

(6) In the large cutters—23-metres and "J" Class—in the old days of the three headsail rig, we always took in the jib topsail first. This sail was set on the longest stay of the vessel, and when it started to blow this stay sagged to leeward so that the luff and clew were both parallel to the centre-line and all this sail was doing was heeling the vessel and pushing her sideways to leeward and not ahead. A sail that has no angle to the centre-line cannot deflect the wind aft and so cannot drive ahead, which is why we try to ease our sheets on all possible occasions, knowing that the greater the angle of the sail the greater will be the drive ahead.

E

Any part of the sail parallel to the centre-line presses without driving our boat.

(7) Barges often brailed in their mainsails and kept their topsail, staysail and mizzen set, as the topsail caught the high, true wind aloft and the staysail and mizzen at each end twisted the barge about as required. Generally a yacht would reduce sail at her ends and keep the drive amidships. This has the advantage that if it continues to blow harder the sails in the middle of the see-saw, where the motion is least and the decks widest, are more easily handled and, if necessary, reduced, until finally a schooner may be lying with her head tucked under her wind, under foresail only.

(8) Having developed and perfected the sea-going planing hull we had to develop a new technique of sailing, for whereas in the days of the Gunter rig we could quickly take in a reef for windward work and shake it out off the wind, we cannot do this with the Bermudian rig which has now come to stay. Therefore, I treated my mainsail as a powerful game fish on a light rod and line. The fish must be played in and out so that it never puts a breaking strain on the line, and I planned never to put the capsizing load into the mainsail, but always up to that load, so that on the wind the mainsail was often fluttering like a flag, excepting for the lower after corner. The headsail we kept in tight as I sailed on the luff of this. In order to plane I had to design boats with a firm bilge and Vee sections. Now while this boat was balanced when upright and just a little ardent, squeezing up into the wind she loved, when she heeled too much she became too ardent and needed weather helm. To counterbalance this tendency the headsail was always held taut and the mainsail eased in squalls, so all the while we travelled along at our top speed close-hauled, in spite of using only a quarter of our mainsail in the squalls. Once round the weather mark the Lord put all the wind he had that day into the mainsail and we would lift up our bow and run in a groove perhaps three inches less than our normal draught scuttling along at twice the speed of the normal-shaped boats.

(9) We must always bear in mind that when we sail to windward we increase the wind's speed on our sail by our own speed, and off the wind decrease it by our speed. So we can always carry more sail off the wind than on.

Setting and Handling Sails

In my earlier days, we had sails of flax or cotton, either hand- or machine-sewn. Nowadays, they are generally of cotton, Terylene or Nylon, machine-sewn or welded together with a minimum of hand work. Yet throughout all the years the sail bent correctly on its spars and cared for properly will always beat the one hung up like washing to dry, as the one has great driving power and the other little. Cotton mainsails should be set taut on the boom —just taut enough for the wrinkles in the sail to disappear, no more—then the battens laced in their correct pockets and the sail hoisted on its main halyard, again taut enough to remove all the wrinkles. When stretching new sails they should be taken out on foot and luff gently until quite clear of any creases, and set taut from time to time as required. If not, the boom end will droop and put unfair strains on the sail.

If we sail through the night we must always bear in mind that the night air and dew will shrink a sail. In *Fresh Breeze* we let the maintack tackle go at sunset. Through the night the boom used to lift gently and quietly as the sail shrank and the luff shortened with the dew. By morning the boom would have risen as much as twelve inches, which shows the care that should be taken to ease in sails when wet.

Now when your mainsail is finally stretched and set out on its spars it should last for twenty years, but in racing we all tend to get new sails before we need them. As a sail stretches it gets flatter, the round goes out of it and also its leech. There is exactly the same amount of material in the sail as before, but now it is in different places. If you stretch a piece of elastic it gets longer and narrower, but there is no more material in it. So it is with a sail stretched : it sets flatter and is better in a breeze of wind for being flat.

A great deal has been written and said about full sails and their drive, but yarning some years ago on this subject with Sir Ralph Gore, Commodore of the Royal Yacht Squadron and President of the R.Y.A., who through a long sailing life in all classes of vessels has gained great knowledge, we both agreed that we had never lost a race through a flat sail, but we had lost many through too full a sail. So, if in doubt, put up a flat sail.

In the old days almost all cutters, large or small, had a three headsail rig, jib topsail, jib, and staysail. In 1934 Frances Herreshoff of America, son of the famous Nathaniel Herreshoff who turned back so many of our America's Cup challengers, designed a two-headsail rig for the "J"-Boat *Whirlwind*. It was a bold and prophetic design, for until then all these large cutters had the three-headsail rig, so today's masts have a 33 per cent increased loading.

When we set our sails and sail our vessels we must always bear in mind that nowadays all the masts are supported by a system of wire rigging with very little stretch in it, and almost all these shrouds and stays run down to the deck over crosstrees to give them a better angle of support. As well as this there is the mainsheet from the end of the mainboom well aft.

This means that our vessel is like a bow, the mast like the arrow and the rigging like the bowstring, and several things happen: first of all the wire stretches and gives just a little; secondly, the mast which is a strut under compression, shortens a little; and then the hull itself bends to the strains. On the weather side the sheer strake and the deck tend to lift, if only a fraction, to the pull on the main shrouds and runners; then the stemhead lifts with the strain from the jib and forestays, and farther aft, when the mainsheet is hove down tight and the runners are set up taut with full load in them, the stern of the vessel lifts as well. Meanwhile, on the leeside, there is a great pressure upward of water supporting the vessel and stopping her from going down on her beam ends. All these things cause the lee rigging of a vessel to be slack and to swing about, for no matter how much you tighten up your mast and rig, once you start sailing hard the lee rigging becomes slack, which itself tells you that all these things are happening. In some vessels the boat bends a great deal and in others it is the mast shortening. This varies with every mast, every rig and every vessel, but it is a combination of all these factors that lets the jibstay and the forestay sag away to leeward to the detriment of the headsails.

As there is bound to be a sag in the headstays it naturally follows that the longer the stay and the longer the sail the greater the sag. That is why, in the old days the jib topsail was always the first sail to be taken in on a wind and why today, with a masthead rig, the jib should be the first sail to be reduced in size. In other words, the first reef is by changing from a large jib down to a smaller one, and then to a smaller one—before ever reefing the mainsail or reducing the area of the staysail. Sail areas should be reduced in this way until finally a masthead cutter is sailing with her staysail and reefed mainsail only. For, as the forestay is much shorter than the jibstay from the stemhead to the masthead, there is less sag in this stay, and, moreover, it is lower on the mast and on a stronger place. It is also farther inboard on a stronger place of the hull and so takes a great deal of the load off mast and hull as well as the rig. On top of this the sails are now farther inboard where the motion is least and the decks wider and safer to work from.

Light Weather Sails

In calms and light airs we set jibs and possibly mainsails of the lightest material so that they may catch the zephyrs which can fully extend this cobweb of sail and let the vessel ghost along. These sails are often called "ghosters". But we must beware of the least increase in wind, for even in light breezes these light sails go into a great big bag and tend to drag the boat to leeward instead of driving her ahead. So these light sails are often set flying with the next heavier sail set in stops on the stay ready to break out in an instant when the "ghoster" can be hauled down. A "ghoster" is often with advantage a fairly small sail, otherwise there is so much area in it that the wind fails to extend the great mass of sail, no matter how light its material, and its object is defeated by its bulk.

Needless to say, the sheets attached to such a sail should also be of the lightest material, otherwise they drag the clew into the side of the vessel and defeat the purpose of this light sail. Many people put heavy metal clips on these sheets so that they can be changed, but I like to see light sheets spliced straight into the clew. Directly the wind gets too strong for the sheet to bear the strain, the sail should come in and be finished with. And if the sheet is still wet it can easily be coiled up clear of the sail and the sail put in its sailbag while the sheet is left outside to dry.

There is a wonderful little rope works in Cowes—Bannisters— that before the war used to make and ship out the mainsheets for the America's Cup defenders. This was in three sizes and so three times the normal length; it was robust and the right size for hard-weather sailing at one end and there was enough of it to be played in and out to the full extent in heavy weather. Now the sheet was tapered down to where it was only strong enough for a light breeze, and again was the full length. After this it was tapered still more so that it was quite thin and very light, and again the full length. With such a mainsheet the skipper could reel it off to suit the weather. If he started off with only little cat's paws on the water he would have the thin sheet working away and as the breeze freshened through the day he would haul in and use a larger size, and then in the afternoon when the breeze came true and strong, as usually happens, he would haul away and bring in the heavy-weather mainsheet. It was all very easily and quietly done, as all these mainsheets were doubled-ended and you only had to ease away on one and haul away on another of this continuous long sheet to get whichever size you wanted in action.

It may seem wrong to have three times the length of sheet you need in a vessel, but you must have one strong enough to stand up to hard-weather sailing, and the other two extra lengths made into this particular sheet during the manufacture were all so much thinner that there was very little weight in them, they took up very little space, and were well worth their weight and place aboard such a vessel. Many a race was won because you could change from a heavy-weather to a light-weather, or "ghosting", sheet without ever having to unreeve. You could never be caught by surprise; you quietly hauled in without altering the trim of your mainsail and used whatever sheet best suited the weather.

So we should have sheets to suit the various weather conditions and remember that if we attach light sheets with spring clips that weigh quite a bit we increase the weight on the clew and so pull the clew of the sail into the side of the boat, whereas we know full well that the farther we can get the clew of our headsails or any other sail, away from our vessel, the more drive ahead there is in the sail. A glance at photographs of any sailing boat show that the clew of all the headsails and the spinnakers tends to pull in towards the side of the boat. In many cases a clew is turned in towards the boat, which means that this part of the sail is pushing the boat backwards. For in order to drive a boat ahead the sail must be at an angle from the stemhead outwards from the lee side and any part of the sail that is parallel to the centre-line is pressing the boat without driving it ahead or astern. And any part of a sail that is curving in backwards to the centre-line is driving the boat astern. All this cannot be emphasised too much.

Light-Weather Sailing

The great thing is to keep your boat moving through the water. Never attempt to sail really tight up on the wind, but to sail more water and keep her footing as fast as possible, so you will seldom be sailing close-hauled, but one point free of this, sailing a greater distance searching for more wind. When you put her through the wind on to the other tack, do it as slowly and as quietly as you can, for it is surprising how long a boat will carry her way with gentle use of the rudder.

Some years ago there was a Royal Southern race from the mouth of the Hamble river to Poole. With hardly any wind my 20-tonner, *Fresh Breeze*, left late so we had to use the 15-h.p. motor all the way across the Solent. As we approached the starting-line the 10-minute flag broke out with the flash and smoke of the gun, followed later by its sound—for sound takes some five seconds to travel a mile. We were still some way off, so we started our stopwatches, kept our engine running and then, thirty seconds before the five-minute signal, the Blue Peter and gun, we stopped the engine (for now we were under the racing rules). *Fresh Breeze* gradually became slower and slower, although we kept her sails full of the light air, and we arrived in amongst the other competitors and on the right side of the line a minute before the starting-gun. We still had steerage way and still had control, for I had used the rudder as little as possible all through this long period, and we slid over the line at its windward end and into first place, and continued out and down the Solent, rounding the different marks called for in the programme before making any Westing. We were out ahead of the fleet and, picking up little cat's paws here and there, worked right away from them all. *Fresh Breeze* was, in fact, the only vessel to get to Poole that night, and so won this cup.

So in all light-weather sailing it is of the utmost importance to handle your sails gently, your rudder gently and your vessel gently, and to move as quietly and calmly as you can about the decks, keeping as low as possible so that every breath of air goes into the sails and is not stopped by human beings acting as windbreaks. Light-weather sailing calls for the utmost skill and patience. Anyone can sail in the ordinary weight of wind, 12 to 18 m.p.h.; it is only in the extremes of weather, both light and heavy, that the experienced helmsman and seaman comes to the fore and into his own, for now the conditions are difficult and all his accumulated knowledge of sailing and seamanship is at his fingertips to be used at every moment.

In the three Atlantic crossings I made in small sailing vessels, I took charge of the mast and its rigging and the trimming of sails. Every fine day I would go aloft and look over every bolt, fitting, shackle, wire and attachments. Then, knowing the habits of all the things aloft, I could rest content on deck when hard weather came, and once the storm was over, check up again on everything aloft. I spent a great deal of time looking up the track on the back edges of masts to see how much they bent fore and aft and how much they were affected by the vessel plunging into a heavy sea, and also going out on the stemhead or bowsprit and looking up the jib and forestays to see how much sag there was in these. The method I used for measuring the bend in the mast was to gauge this by the diameter of the mast at a place I knew. It could be a quarter, a half, or a whole diameter of the mast, and in this way I knew the exact amount of bend and whip.

For measuring the sag in the headstays I used the same system we use in describing a distant object to a man, when we stretch our arm out to its full length and then put up one, two, three or four fingers, or a whole hand and say that the object is one or more fingers to the right of something very conspicuous, as this enables the next person to pick up this difficult object quite swiftly. So what I do is to put my arm out at full length and put up one, two, or three fingers to measure the sag in the headstays of the vessel. Generally speaking, the best-rigged vessels have a two-finger sag in their forestay, and this sag is to leeward and aft, for the stay is pulled in the direction of the luff of the sail, almost always at an angle of 45° from the centre-line of the ship. So if you have a two-finger sag in your forestay you haven't got much to worry about. But if it is more, then you should set a smaller jib to reduce the sag in the stay and the efficiency of the jib. This reduction in sail will not only increase the efficiency of your jib and vessel, but because your vessel is not being so heavily pressed by useless sail she will be more upright, and the more upright a vessel is the faster she will slide through the water. Once a vessel is heeled— and the beamier the vessel the truer this is—her lines are distorted, the weather lines becoming finer and the lee lines coarser. Many people think that all the fuss and boil on the lee side of a vessel is speed, but actually the more the fuss, quite often the less the speed.

Sail Trimming

When we are on a wind or reaching, it is the jib or staysail that is cutting into the clean air. So this is the first sail to adjust. You trim this in with its sheet so that it is set as perfectly as possible, and the jib sheet generally should drop about 5° from the mitre seam of the side. Then you move the lead forward and aft slightly so that the foot and the leech both flutter and lift at the same time, for if the sheet lead is too far aft the foot becomes hard and flat and if it is too far forward the leech becomes straight and hard, throwing the wind from the headsail straight into the mainsail. As a rough rule it would be better to have the foot tighter and the leech a little more flowing, so that this flat, hard leech does not throw the wind straight back into the mainsail. We must remember that the mainsail is curved on its lee side and therefore the leech of the jib should go out in the same curve as the mainsail. Often we need to take the jib lead a little farther aft than correct to slacken its leech and let it take up the same curve as the lee side of the mainsail.

Once we have set the headsails as we think best, we can start trimming in our mainsheet and make the final adjustment between all the sails so that all lift on their luffs at exactly the same moment. Most people hate to see a fluttering leech, but by the time the wind has reached the back edge of the sail it has finished its work and now must be allowed to escape off a slack leech. There must be a correct angle for this, and so if the leech is just fluttering slightly it means that twice in every flutter it is at the most perfect angle for letting the wind go off the sail; I have never lost a race yet through a slack leech, but I have lost many through a tight one.

In 1928, when I had the International 14-footer *Avenger*, we were for the first time allowed Bermudian masts, and as usual that year Ratseys & Lapthorn of Cowes had more work than they could possibly cope with in the early part of the summer. Consequently, they were unable to make my new mainsail and jib and I had to race with a gunter lug mainsail set on a Bermudian mast. This sail shook and fluttered on the leech, but in spite of this I won the first eleven races, and was winning the twelfth with quite a comfortable lead when I saw the late beloved Tom Ratsey aboard *Dolly Varden* on his mooring in Cowes Roads watching and enjoying the racing going on all around. I made a tack to sail close by and said, "Don't you feel sorry for me? Look at this shaking leech." He stood up in the cockpit and with a chuckle said, "You've got a long lead, long enough to tack and come and talk to me. You needn't worry, I've never seen a race lost yet through a slack leech." So on I sailed after a couple of tacks alongside him, and we won this race as well. *Avenger* won her first twenty races, using a gunter lug mainsail on a Bermudian mast with a shaking leech.

Ever since then I have never taken a pull at a leech line of headsails or mainsails but always encourage them to flutter, though not enough to disturb the whole sail, for this disturbs the wind, not only of the headsail, but of the mainsail as well, and it is then difficult to tell when you are on a wind or off if going to windward. So all sails should be trimmed and arranged so that their leeches have just the least flutter in them, with their luffs standing taut and bold.

Most vessels have their headstays double the strength of the halyards, and these halyards, when hove up by winches as they are today, should never take more strain than the headstay itself. We should see that the strain on the halyard and on the headstay is equal and no more. We now have our luffs set to perfection and because all the halyard is of wire we do not have to keep on jigging it up as we did in the old days with rope tails. However, most headsails and mainsails require constant sheeting even after being trimmed to perfection because of continuous stretch and give in the rope sheets.

A great many people have wire sheets, but these are brutal things to handle. The man wrapping the jibsheet round the winch can often get his finger in as well, and fingers have been nipped off before now. This always stops the race, for you must take such a man to hospital quickly as there is no enjoyment for anyone on board until he is in hospital. So rather than risk cutting a finger off with wire sheets, I always use Italian hemp or Terylene, as these have terrific strength and are easily handled. If they do snarl up they can be cut free fairly simply, and although if they hit you they give you a good whack, they do not cut off the fingers or ears. I am surprised that the I.Y.R.U., the Royal Ocean Racing Club and the Cruising Club of America do not forbid wire jib and mainsheets and so safeguard those racing under their rules.

Sailing to Windward

When racing in strong breezes and heavy winds we must always carry more sail to windward than our boat can really bear. There are several reasons for this: although she is overpowered in the squalls and sometimes wallows and slows down there are many lulls between the squalls and in this she will be travelling at her top speeds. If we are skilful we can also keep our vessel travelling at her top speed through the gusts, and gain on those who have less sail because of our higher speed between the squalls.

We must remember that once any person with normal intelligence has sailed for several hours he can sail a boat as well as anyone in a 15-m.p.h. wind. But what wins races and gets a good cruising man to his harbour while others are still miles out behind and probably being overtaken by a storm, is not just sailing ability, but concentration on things such as wind shifts, different strengths in the same wind, the run of the tidal streams, how to take a boat over a wave, and a thousand and one little things like that.

When after three years I had developed and perfected the planing lines of little sea-going boats in *Avenger*, I had another great problem. Under me I had a design that, with its deep chest and Vee sections running right aft, lifted out on top of the water and would go double the speed of normal boats, planing away with a strong wind abeam to the quarter. But though quite fast on a dead run, because of her smallness and the awkwardness of the seas, she seldom planed running at sea, although she wanted to and often did in smoother water.

At this time the Bermudian mast had come in and, whereas until then we had reefed our gunter lug sails and at the same time reefed our spars, with a Bermudian rig although you reef your sail you do not reef the mast, and this great, long spar sticking up above the sail punishes the boat almost as much as full sail. So I had to develop a technique of sailing that would allow me to carry full sail to windward so that I might have it for planing off the wind.

We would keep our jib sheeted home for close-hauled work, and as the squalls came I would play the mainsheet in and out so that we would be using the whole, three-quarters, half, or only a quarter, or perhaps none of the mainsail during this squall. Often I have been going along at top speed close-hauled for a matter of thirty seconds in the fiercest part of the squall with the mainsail fluttering throughout like a flag. But even so I suppose there was still a little drive in it; anyway it kept the boat on her feet so she did not heel, scooping water to leeward and slowing herself down through making the leeward lines coarse, and so we would battle our way to windward with all this amount of sail.

One of the great arts of this is to watch the sky to see when a heavy cloud is coming and to remember that, just as rain dropping from a cloud only hits you when the cloud is overhead although it descended from the cloud itself perhaps a mile to windward of you, so it is with the wind. It does not strike you until the cloud is overhead, although the wind of the cloud that you are now feeling left the cloud a mile or so earlier. So you watch the clouds and, if you also watch the water to windward, you will be able to see an oncoming squall rippling and ruffling the surface of the sea, and will be ready to ease your sheet as it strikes your little boat.

In larger vessels, twenty-tonners and above, powerful ships with half their weight in their keels low down, you haven't got the manpower on board to play the mainsheet in and out for squalls. So what I do in vessels like these is again to watch the clouds and the surface of the sea for squalls and as they take hold start to sail her just a little finer and squeeze her up a quarter of a point, or more, all depending on the fineness of the lines.

When doing this it is no good looking at a speedometer. These are far too slow, with the exception of one, to note any change in speed, and you must watch the waters swirling past your vessel (actually it is of course the boat going through the sea) and have the general feel of the boat on her rudder. For even with a wheel, your ship will still talk to you up through her rudder if you only allow her to and listen intently. Then you do not get knocked down by these squalls, you do not slow up; in fact you gain a little over the other man because you are now sailing a touch higher. But this demands a great deal of skill, and you must have sailed the boat a fair amount hard on the wind in a breeze to get the feel and knowledge of her required to take her through heavy squalls.

Sailing With a Free Wind Across the Tide

Most places—be they inland rivers, estuaries, or the sea itself—have currents or tides to contend with, and one of the difficult things in a place such as the Solent is to go reaching across the tide for a mark sometimes out of sight down under the horizon. For if a mark is four miles away the curvature of the earth will hide it from a man in a small boat, and he has to judge where his mark is and steer a steady course for it. You can steer off the wind in almost any compass direction, but the point you want to steer on is one that will, with due allowance for the tide, take you steadily and directly towards the mark. For the shortest distance is a straight line and to follow it you must watch the land beyond the shore and see that your bearing does not change. You get a tree and a house, or possibly a cow and a hayrick, and keep these in line, and so long as they remain in line you know you are steering a steady course.

Naval men are really good at this, and of any I have ever seen Prince Philip is the most expert at this sort of sailing. For when we are on such a course we trim our sails, set our spinnaker and trim that, and we never have to change the trim because he has changed his compass direction. Most people on such a course are continually altering direction, which means the sails are constantly

losing their wind and you are forever altering the sheeting angle;
all of this, of course, slows a vessel up.

Centreboards or Drop-Keels

To windward the drop-keel in a good breeze of wind should be
lowered to its limit, to give you the maximum grip on the water
and the greatest depth in order to stop you sliding to leeward.
With the wind abeam you can raise the keel to about an angle of
45° and so reduce its underwater area by about one third. For
running you should pull it well up but always have the area of the
rudder in the drop-keel exposed. Some people pull them right up,
but this is a great mistake for when you start using rudder, as you
must do, the whole of your boat skids and slides about on the
water and fairly soon you discover you have capsized.

Even rowing eights, which are circular in section and where every
effort has been made to cut down wetted surface, have little metal
fins about three-quarters of their length from the fore end for the
rudders to act upon. So you must have some drop-keel down as a
fin to give your rudder something positive to act upon, otherwise
you will skid about on the water like a car on a greasy road. So
always, when off the wind, reduce your wetted area by pulling up
as much drop-keel as possible, but in purely drop-keel boats never
pull it up completely. This does not apply to the semi-drop-keel
boats, those with an iron shoe or a wooden fin underneath them
through which the drop-keel works, for this fixed fin itself acts as a
little skeg for the rudder to work upon.

In England we call the men who work on farms "farm labour-
ers", but very few people on earth have to know more than the
farm labourer. Generally speaking he does every job once a year.
He ploughs and plants various things, tends them as they grow,
cuts and gathers them in for the winter, and does thousands of
things just once a year. But there are many things to be done daily,
and some twice daily, such as milking cows, feeding and caring for
the various animals, and the farm labourer must store up in his
mind a great deal of knowledge of all these things, many of which
only happen once a year. So it is with the seaman. He must know
—for at sea there is no time to explain—things which may have to
be done as swift as light, and it takes years to make a good seaman

whose knowledge of all the problems at sea is infinite. Yet the more we understand and know, the more we can enjoy the pure magic of sailing.

Spinnakers

Spinnakers are set from their three corners only. They are great balloon-like sails and we can learn something about their handling and setting every time we use them. So here are a few points to bear in mind about these exciting sails, full of fun but troublesome.

In my drawing office at Cowes I have a lovely coloured print of the *Arrow* winning a Royal London Yacht Club race in the 1850's. She is coming up to the mark boat with her mainsail and topsail stretched out all a-taut before a heavy breeze, her spinnaker boom well squared off and set on this, and filling all the gap to the hounds (jib halyard height) is a low set spinnaker. Above this is set another spinnaker in the form of a great jib topsail, again from the spinnaker boom end but now to the topmast head. So her spinnaker is set in two halves. Away back behind is a second cutter roaring along with a great single spinnaker, and what I imagined to have happened that day was that the famous *Arrow* sailed down the West, rounded the weather mark with a good lead and, because of wind, decided to set a small spinnaker for the run home. The second boat, rounding astern, decided that she would never catch the *Arrow* with a small spinnaker so set her great spinnaker which forced *Arrow* to set a second sail over her lowcut spinnaker. And so, with the same sail area but in two pieces, she continued and won the race.

Whether this was so or not, it is an idea for ocean racers which often have to make a decision and never know if it is the right one. For they can, as proved by this painting, set a small spinnaker and then set a longer luff one above it. This has several advantages. First, the same sail area goes up in two pieces which makes it easier to handle, both setting, sheeting and getting in at the end. Second, it spreads the load over the mast so that there is little chance of carrying away any gear or the mast. And third, if the weather increased they could take in either one and so reduce their area and risk quite easily. So we never cease to learn and wonder over spinnakers.

Nowadays we set our spinnaker booms well up the mast and this means that the fore guy and the after guy are both pulling downwards and so act as a downhaul from the end of the boom, taking all the strains off it. In the old days we used to set our spinnaker, and if it was lifting too much and demanded a downhaul on the spinnaker boom, we would ease away on the spinnaker halyard until the top of the spinnaker was exactly over its foot. This meant that it was neither lifting nor pressing and would fly out steadily straight ahead of the boat. This little trick has been lost sight of in the years that have passed, but it is well worth remembering, as it is quite a seamanlike thing to do.

I like to have a stop on my spinnaker halyard to prevent my pulling the head close into the mast as is always done these days, for when the spinnaker head is close into the mast it has several disadvantages. The foot must now be forward of it and this means that the spinnaker is lifting and skying and putting a great deal of strain on to the spinnaker boom by trying to lift it up in the air. It also means that the spinnaker head is tight into the mainsail, choking itself and the mainsail, and not allowing either to work properly because of the trapped air swirling around. Whereas, if you free the spinnaker head away from the mast it will almost always pull out away from the mast and give you a more effective spinnaker area and a greater spread to your spinnaker luff, as it flies out away from the mast and the boat itself.

In a Flying Fifteen this wants to be 18 in. to 2 ft. in length, and in larger vessels more. It has a further advantage, for many of these larger vessels have their jib and spinnaker halyard at 80% of their mast height, so have to have jumper struts and stays. These wire stays chafe through the spinnaker and its stitching and quite often tear it, whereas if you ease away on your halyard the sail flies out clear of the jumper struts, and as the top part of the spinnaker halyard is generally wire, it means that there are two wires rubbing against each other and they take a long time to do any damage. So everything points to the spinnaker head being free of the mast and never choked in close to it.

Another thing we must do with a spinnaker, especially when we are reaching with the wind abeam, is to keep the boom end high. This slackens up the foreward leech or the luff of the spinnaker and

This International One-Design has her mainsheet eased off so far that the mainsail is forward of the mast at the top. Since this is where pressure and leverage are greatest, the vessel develops a tremendous weather-roll, making life miserable on board. The remedy is to haul in on the mainsheet to bring the mainsail square athwartships at the top (see page 64).

The spinnakers on these 6-Metres are so large that they are set on all possible occasions; but the windward boat with her genoa jib set is going just as fast as the other two, because the greater part of their sails that is curved backward is slowing them down.

Sherry Spinner's mainsheet is eased off so much that the mainsail is pressing against the jumper struts; this means it is 35° forward of the mast, which accounts for the violent weather roll. But her spinnaker is set to perfection, while the furthest Dragon has hers flying too high and has lost a quarter of its area.

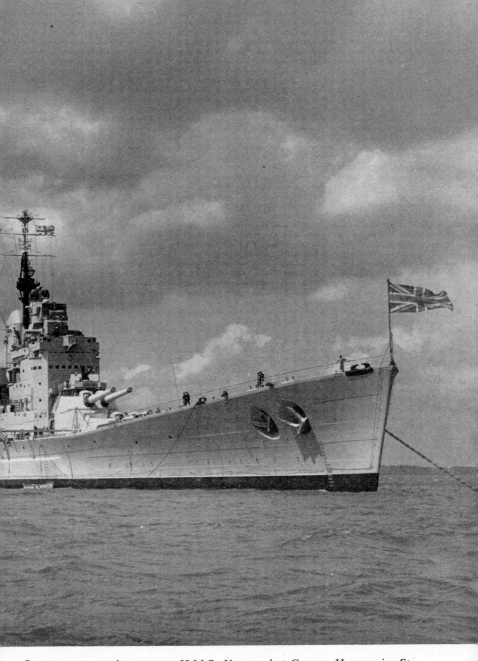

Ocean racers coming up past H.M.S. *Vanguard* at Cowes. Here again, *St. Barbara* (*nearest to the camera*) is flying her spinnaker far too high; it is large enough to reach the water, so a third of its area is being wasted.

The German *Rubin*, a great ocean racer, running by the lee almost on the point of a gybe. The spinnaker is giving her a weather roll, because the wind coming across her port quarter is filling it without exerting any pressure at all in the mainsail.

Navahoe leading *Calluna, Iverna* and *Satanita*. Since she has come all the way across the Atlantic to race here, we may be sure that everything possible has been done to put her into fighting trim; and yet she has an enormous sag in her jib topsail, and the other vessels have too. No wonder this was the first sail stowed with a rising wind, for it only presses such vessels to leeward.

This is the earliest picture of a sea-going boat planing over the top of the water. The sail is piled on to give the power that lifts *Daring* out of the sea, leaving a wake like a destroyer.

sends it a long way to leeward, which in turn means that the clew of your spinnaker is a long way to leeward of the mainsail and in no danger of backwinding it. Moreover, all that part of the spinnaker turning in towards the boat on its after edge is driving the boat backwards and not ahead. So it is always better to have your spinnaker luff well away to leeward and your spinnaker boom end a little farther forward than you really think is necessary, as this in turn takes the leech and clew of the spinnaker away to leeward and clear of the mainsail.

The vast majority of people with spinnakers think that as long as they are full of wind they are working. They are, but not to their utmost, and I have won many and many a race by keeping the spinnaker luff on edge, so that it is always slightly collapsing, as unless it is continually fluttering you have your sheet too tight without realising it, your vessel is sheet bound, and the spinnaker tends to heel the boat and stop her rather than lift and push her ahead over the glad waters.

During the Cowes Week of 1959, the Duke of Edinburgh's Flying Fifteen *Coweslip* was champion of the Week. This was often due to our spinnaker being on edge and continually fluttering on its luff and lifting our boat along just a little faster than the others, whose spinnakers were all hard and full of wind and appeared to be working, but in actual fact were pressing rather than driving the boats to the utmost. So you must continually strive to get the clew of your spinnaker away to leeward and a long way away from the mainsail, as once it starts choking the mainsail with its head and clew, it will stop and stun your boat.

The golden rule of all sailing is to free all your sheets and get your sails off the centre-line as much as possible, but this rule is more true of spinnakers than of any other sail, so never be content when your spinnaker is full of wind; keep its luff on edge and fluttering all the time so that it lifts your boat over the waters to its utmost.

Sailing in Waves

Almost every boat steers easily in smooth water. In the first place, at sea the wind is gentle and her passage through the water quiet so there are no pressures or strains. But even at sea you sometimes get a strong offshore wind with smooth water when squalls

F

will heel your boat over. And most boats on heeling start to carry weather helm and try to luff up into the wind. Once a boat gets out of the upright she becomes unbalanced and the more she is driven out of the upright the more unbalanced she becomes. Helm must be applied to correct this.

There are, of course, boats which, on heeling over, carry lee helm. In the 1880's, because of the tonnage rule, yachts were built long and narrow, for length gave speed and the narrow beam gave a low tonnage and a good handicap. I sailed from Brightlingsea on the east coast in an exact replica of the old three-tonner *La Mascotte*. We left in a strong northerly, and with full sail made a very fast passage for a three-tonner to Cowes, 200 miles in 23 hours, an average of over 8½ knots.

Through the Swatchways, between the sands in the Thames Estuary, I constantly looked at the chart as she ran with a high quarter wave that roared like an express train. It was just such a wave as a normal vessel pulls up sailing over shallow ground, but this was a feature of these boats and I grew accustomed to it as the miles reeled by. She sailed quite comfortably until we rounded the South Foreland and started along the south coast. Now we had the wind abeam, and the hard squalls pulling off the land knocked her over on her beam ends and laid her out flat in the water in spite of her lead keel low down.

After passing the Owers, we had to steer N.W. hard on the wind, and now I discovered why she had a great wishbone tiller. When she was heeled she had the terribly dangerous habit of carrying lee helm, and in the hard squalls, with the water halfway up her deck and her lead keel ploughing through the fresh air in the hollow of the bow and stern waves on her weather side, I would have my arm and shoulder under water, although I was holding the weather side of the wishbone. The tiller was down at an angle of 45° in an effort to keep her from running off the wind and being put more and more on her beam ends. So where weather helm makes hard work in a boat, it also makes for safety; whereas lee helm is most dangerous.

This will illustrate what you can do in the way of avoiding waves and seas providing you have a very quick vessel under you that is light and buoyant, able to twist and turn without losing way, and one you have sailed thousands of miles in, so that you know everything there is to know about her and you—your boat and your mind have all been welded into one unit.

I used to play centre-half at soccer and only once have I seen the opportunity to take the ball single-handed half the length of the pitch and score. The enemy's defences were so disposed that with a bit of swerving I cut clean through the lot and finally banged the ball into the net. A few moments of glorious excitement and a wonderful feeling of exaltation at the end, although my job was to stop the other team playing football, not to score goals. Years ago I had this same exciting and elated feeling with the little 22-square metre *Vigilant*, whose dimensions describe her liveliness.

Length Overall: 34′ 6″ (10·515m)   *Length Waterline:* 25′ 6″ (7·772m)
Beam: 6′ 4″ (1·930m)   *Draught:* 4′ 3″ (1·295m)
Displacement: 2 *tons* (2,032 *kilos*) *Sail Area:* 236 *sq. ft.* (22 *sq. m*)

Her displacement was less than half that of a 6-metre, and her hull only extended 18 in. below the waterline, the rest of her draft being in her short fin keel; so she was an extreme type of racing vessel. She had the ability to twist and turn like a swallow and as I had cruised in her from Cowes to Stockholm in the Baltic and back, and made other fairly long voyages as well as racing her, I knew her every movement. Now I had sold her and was taking her to her new owner in Torquay, and we had arrived on the lee side of Portland Bill in a strong westerly wind with a spring ebb under us. This is what the Pilot Book says:

"RACE OF PORTLAND. The tide runs with great violence round the Bill and over the ledge, causing fearful whirls and eddies in its progress; but there is generally an eddy of still water, a quarter of a mile wide, between the Race and the land. During Spring tides, which run at the rate of 5 or 6 knots, the agitation is so violent in the Race as to render it *dangerous for small vessels*; and in tempestuous weather, during the northeastern stream, the whole space between Portland and the Shambles is one sheet of broken water."

With our small sail area I decided that, as I had Bob with me who had sailed to Sweden and back, I would lash myself in the cockpit, which was self-bailing, while he would be down below as we took her through the Race just for the sheer joy of it, watching out through the portholes on either side of the coach roof, knowing full well he could not be swept overboard and could come out immediately there was any trouble. With this slashing breeze we soon cleared the smooth water inside the Race and then we were in amongst great, tumbling seas. Pyramids of water, with no shape form, or reason, they were like the rapids of a swift-flowing river, further agitated by the strong wind against the 6-knot tidal stream.

My plan was exactly as it was when I ran the ball right through the defences of the enemy at Soccer. It was to take avoiding action swiftly and continue on my way without ever pausing or losing any way, for once we lost way in this turmoil any sea would crash aboard. Our safety lay in high speed and using it to avoid the worst of the breaking crests, and the task was made even more difficult by seas which quite often would suddenly explode under and near us, thrown upwards as if by some gigantic undersea explosion. I watched the waves and their formation and sometimes was close-hauled and sometimes had the wind right out on the quarter, sailing round the base of these mountains of water without being on the top or in the way of their great crashing, curling crests.

They were some of the most exciting minutes I ever had sailing. Every so often a sea would crash aboard unexpectedly, but the boat was so light and buoyant and her decks so small that it quickly ran off. So we drove through the Race with a 6-knot tide taking us on our way plus our own speed, as for the main part we sailed close-hauled and only went off course to avoid the terrifying breakers. Finally, the sea stopped exploding under us and the fearful whirls, eddies, and overfalls gave way to a more regular sea. We were through into the Channel sea, which, although breaking and fairly large, because of its rhythm and regularity now seemed sensible and sane and easy to ride over by comparison.

When in various yacht clubs I listen to the hard-bitten cruising men, plumb stem and stern sort of chaps, who dislike overhangs and light displacement. I seldom if ever argue with them. It is usually a pure waste of time and, wherever you are, if you listen you stand a chance of learning, but if you talk you can never learn anything. And so I listen and by being patient often learn something from these chaps, but I still feel sorry for them because they

have missed all the joy of the swallow's swift and easy motion and
are convinced that the only way to sail is to lumber along like a
rook.

When driving to windward in a big sea, where some of the seas
and their great breaking crests are more than your vessel can
endure, nine out of ten people luff their vessels into this oncoming
sea. This to my mind is a mistake and I bear away and take that
same sea abeam. If we luff into a big sea, we rush straight at it and
our own speed adds to the force of the wave; moreover, we are
now climbing directly up the steep face of the sea which of course,
hits us with even more violence, often sweeping our decks and
always knocking all the way off our vessel. What I have always
done for every seventh sea, with its great breaking crest, is to bear
away and take it right abeam. Now your vessel is not adding her
own speed to the violence of the waves, and because she is heeled
away to leeward, her great round bilge on the weather side is up in
the air, and almost all these waves, taken this way, glide and pass
harmlessly under your vessel, lifting her as they go.

Two incidents will illustrate this. We were sailing the 45-foot
schooner *Diablesse* across the Atlantic. I was aloft looking over
her rigging. On this particular day we were close-hauled in a
strong breeze with quite a sea running, and as usual I had gone up
the mainmast, and instead of coming on deck was ready to go from
one mast to the other upside down, on the triatic stay, using the
backs of my legs and my hands as I was suspended to travel
between the two masts on this stay, which had a slight run down-
hill forward. As usual, I yelled out to the helmsman, "Right, take
the sea abeam, I'm going across!", and directly I saw the seas running abeam I started on my way across and was about halfway
when, just for fun, those on deck started luffing and told me so.
Although this was a dangerous thing I had been crossing on this
stay almost every day for two months at sea and we were all young
and full of fun, and even I did not feel it dangerous. I could see a
fairly large sea coming that we were bound to hit when finally we
came up close-hauled with a lot of way on, and so I started moving
across the last half of that stay as fast as I could. I did not quite
make it before the sea hit us. I tried to hold on but slid with a
swish some eight or nine feet, tucked my head in so that I took the

jolt on the mast with my shoulders, and was in too much pain to look over all the gear on the foremast head. I only did what I could do while sitting on the triatic stay, and came painfully down on deck.

The grooves cut in my hands and the backs of my legs stopped all of us from ever doing that again, and brought home to us the enormous difference in the striking power of a wave when taken with full way on at the 45° close-hauled angle, and when taken abeam when the speed of your ship does not increase the striking power of the wave.

On another occasion we were sailing the International 14-foot dinghy *Avenger* from Cowes to Havre—a distance of 100 miles— in one of our strong south-westers of July—a summer gale. Once we cleared Bembridge Ledge and the Island, with a big and spiteful sea running, we reefed our mainsail down to the crosstree and put on a small jib that only came back to the mast. With this we could just lay Havre comfortably close-hauled on the starboard tack. Even so, the flying spray coming aboard meant continual baling and we knew that we should be exhausted before we reached France, although there were three of us in the boat as I had taken an extra man for strength, stability and baling. So we eased our sheets and took her away from the wind a little; and now we were sailing fairly dry in this light, buoyant boat, which lifted so swiftly to every sea. For at this angle we were not meeting the seas so steeply but were now going at a flatter angle from crest to valley; neither were we meeting them so often, nor was the speed of our vessel increasing the impact of each wave by so much. So we sailed more comfortably, and when we were halfway across Channel and the Cherbourg peninsula, although some fifty miles to windward, started to make its presence felt, we came up on to the wind a little more and made Havre without tacking and arrived intact.

So my advice for sailing to windward in a heavy sea is not to luff into waves and increase their impact and steepness, but to go away from the dangerous waves till they and the wind are abeam. This is easier and safer for the vessel, and although every seventh wave is a large one and is often followed by another immediately on its heels, the crests of waves do not break continually across the ocean and you need only worry about the seventh wave that is going to break dangerously on your vessel, one about every twenty or thirty minutes. I am now talking about a heavy gale with a big sea running out in the open Atlantic. Sailing in a big sea with the wind abeam is a fairly safe operation and there is nothing much you can do anyway, except that if you see a sea that is going to break as it hits you, and you do not want to take it at that moment, you can bear away off course and let it break twenty yards dead to windward of you. But to do this you need a great deal of judgment and anticipation.

When sailing in a big sea on a broad reach with the wind out on your quarter you are on one of the most difficult points of steering, for now the seas come rushing at you in their white shirt-sleeves and strike your weather quarter, giving you a great deal of floatation and buoyancy aft. With the wave level with your deck everywhere, you have probably doubled your buoyancy aft. At the same time, the hollow of the wave is at your stem and it is at this moment that the high-flying stern tends to make the stem dig in; this now has completely unbalanced your boat, and with her forefoot cutting into solid water she will want to gripe and shoot up head to wind. You must anticipate and realise all this and, a fraction of a second before the sea hits you, start applying weather helm to prevent this wild sheer to windward. Once it has started it would be impossible to control, and you would have your vessel flying up into wind and wave with its sail shaking; and broaching-to can be very dangerous, for with a great deal of way on your vessel is slamming herself straight into the oncoming wave and so increasing its power. So driving hard with a quartering sea calls for the utmost skill on the steersman's part and, quite often, he has to exert every ounce of strength he has to control his vessel in these wild, rushing, quartering seas.

Finally, there is running dead before a heavy gale. This is perhaps the most difficult and dangerous of all points of sailing, and you should never run longer than is safe in a heavy gale with a steep following sea. First of all your vessel's weight, if she is of heavy displacement, disturbs the following sea and you can easily get pooped as you pull a great wave right in over your stern. Then the sea just tumbles down, sweeping the deck from aft to forward, carrying everything away and often sweeping people overboard. The Brixham trawlers, wonderful sea boats though they were, had to reduce sail and speed once they reached ten knots before a gale of wind, as this was the speed at which their wake, with their heavy displacement and cargo of fish aboard, disturbed the following seas enough for them to be pooped.

On this point of sailing you have to remember that when you are poised up on the crest of the wave, you are all right. Then you start to rush down its face, which is quite steep, and although you are surf-riding and probably going double your sailing speed, all this broken, boiling water is rushing past you at an even greater pace, so your rudder, or a greater part of it, is useless because the sea is going faster than the rudder and your vessel. Finally, you get at the bottom of this deep valley, between the two waves which seem like the Valley of the Shadow, and your heart has a great many toothmarks on it as you start to dig into the wave ahead. As your bow roots into this and it comes climbing right over the stemhead, your vessel wants to broach-to, and although your rudder now has grip there is still enough speed left in the stern part of your vessel which is still descending to make you twist round and bring wind and sea abeam.

Two incidents will illustrate this danger. Four of us were sailing the 35-foot waterline ketch *Typhoon* across the Atlantic. We had left the Azores and after some thirty days at sea encountered a heavy November gale that wrought havoc amongst big ships. We were out of food and living on flour and water which we made up into little pancakes and had to fry without grease. Being very hungry, our one idea was to drive on at all cost to the American coast and food.

Here we must remember that we are born with two instincts which cause more violence and crime than anything else on this earth; the urge to survive is perhaps the strongest. And we were hungry and hunger has caused revolutions and a great deal of violence in this world. So we drove on before this heavy gale when we knew we should have been hove-to. We sailed past a great three-masted schooner hove-to, taking things comfortably with her head under her wing, while we were carrying a full jib and mizzen. After this, we took in the jib and the mizzen and put up *Dolly Varden*'s tri-sail given to us by the late Tom Ratsey of Cowes, and continued running before this steep sea.

One day we were knocked flat on our beam-ends and lost hal-yards and ropes and everything overboard through broaching in these steep seas. So to steady our ship and to control her when the rudder was useless, we trailed our two great warps astern and these had two effects, they seemed to trip up seas before they struck us with their great length, ironing out the top of the water behind. But their main purpose was this: when we were surging down the breaking seas with our rudder useless because of the water rushing past it and it having very little or no bite these ropes, already thrown forward by the wave some seconds earlier, were now stretched out taut and towing dead astern, steadying our stern and keeping us flying straight. But as the days went by the gale and seas became worse, for it was a heavy winter gale. So, hungry as we were, we knew we had to put our boat's head under her wing, and we decided to heave-to under our sea anchor.

All the halyards were off their belaying-pins and trailing astern. We were in a pretty pickle, and so the four of us came up on deck, ready to take in the tri-sail and stream our sea anchor. We rigged the Voss-type sea anchor and the rope led out through a fairlead on the bowsprit end and aft outside all our rigging, so that when the time came we could throw the sea anchor over from the cock-pit in security and then ease away on this warp as required. Now came the job of getting down the tri-sail. The wind was screeching like a thousand demons as I went forward, hauled the tri-sail hal-yard aboard, coiled it all down and held it securely. Then Jim Dorset started to come forward so that the two of us could haul down the tri-sail. When he was halfway between the two masts we broached-to and a great sea like a mountain thundered aboard. The two in the cockpit were driven tighter into it and Jim, halfway between the two masts and holding on with all his strength, was swept overboard with nothing to grab. And although I held on to the mast with my hands and knees, I also was swept overboard and outwards, but managed to catch hold of the mast well up, for *Typhoon* was not only hove down on her beam ends, but down to an angle of 120°. Fortunately we were all battened down, no water leaked below, and as this sea swept by us, the formation must have been such that we were pushed upright again and I dropped on deck. Then the miracle happened. Although we knew it would take two of us to get the tri-sail down, I managed to get this down by myself. Jim had grabbed one of the ropes trailing astern and was holding on for dear life, although he kept sliding back down it till *Typhoon* lost her way, and at last we had him on our quarter. This was difficult, for although we were now lying without way, our stern would be level with the water and next instant high in the air, and at each surge Jim would slide farther down the rope as we were unable to hold him. In the end I managed to get hold of his oilskins, twist them round and hold them under the inside of the rail. He was pretty red in the face and said I was choking him, but I didn't give a damn about that. We slid a spar under him, pushed down on this like a hand spike, and slid him in sideways over the deck.

We streamed the sea anchor, but we only ever lay to within 45° of the seas and then the warp parted. As we had been lying fairly quietly during this struggle with Jim, because we had no way on, we decided that all we could do was to let *Typhoon* look after herself and lie how she would to wind and sea. We cleaned and tidied the deck and then went below. It was then that we discovered our angle of heel. As we had gone over the inside ballast which was not secured, had burst up the floorboards, then crashed into the chart-table and slid up on to the coach roof. The ashes from our coal fire had dropped across the boat and were under the blankets and bedding of the lee bunk. From this we gauged that we had gone over to an angle of 120°; I never wish to go through such an experience in my life again.

Never run before a heavy gale for longer than your vessel can endure. The heavier the displacement of the vessel the sooner she will have to heave-to, for with a light displacement boat there is no disturbance in the following sea from her wake, as she seems to iron the water out and to quiet down the seas that come chasing after her.

It was in a regatta at Lyme Regis. There was so much wind that the committee postponed the regatta until the afternoon. But the wind and sea had not abated and out we went in the 18-foot Jolly Boat, *Jollity*. It was a close reach out to the first mark and by shaking our mainsail a great deal we managed to carry full sail out to our mark. Then there was a dead run for a buoy under Golden

Cap and because of the weight of the wind we did not set our spinnaker. As we approached the shore the seas grew steeper because of the shallower water and we started to surf down their faces at an ever-increasing speed with each sea.

Nearing the lee buoy we suddenly started to rush at breakneck speed down the face of the waves, surf-riding at an alarming pace. The mainboom came back amidships, for we were now travelling faster than it was blowing, and the rudder became dead and lifeless in my hand. I prayed fervently to the Almighty that *Jollity* would run true and straight, as if she started to sheer the weight of her mast on one side or the other would roll her over. She surfed several times in the two rounds in exactly the same place and I was vastly relieved each time when the wind took hold of the mainsail once again and the rudder started to bite into the water. It is a frightening feeling to be travelling at such a speed in a light, lively centreboard craft, and though we had a good lead, by the time we had righted our boat and straightened her out we might easily have lost it. The wind always lifts over high cliffs long before it reaches them, and so as we were coming into Golden Cap its speed at this point was about 20 m.p.h.—although the wind that day was 25 m.p.h. gusting up to 28—so our surfing speed for those awful quarter or half minutes was something in the region of 20 knots.

So, whether cruising or racing, you must beware of chasing away before wind and sea in blowing weather. It is the most frightening and dangerous of all points of sailing.

IV

The Care of Mast, Rigging and Sails

THE Flying Fifteen has the simplest rig of all and, having chosen her, we now prepare her for sea as she sits on the quay in front of my house. This is only 50 yards away from the inner end of the Island Sailing Club starting-line; 150 yards from the Royal London Yacht Club starting-line; 170 yards from the Royal Corinthian Yacht Club starting-line, and 200 yards from the Royal Yacht Squadron's starting-line. So she sits waiting for us to prepare for sea, surrounded by these great clubs and hundreds of boats to compare her with.

The first thing to do is to look at the tension of the standing rigging of the mast. This must be arranged so that the mast is straight in its athwartships (sideways) direction and straight fore and aft on its after edge in light weather. In blowing weather the rigging should be such that the top of the mast will curve aft and the belly of the mast—halfway between the jib halyard and the deck—bow forward in a gentle curve. This bow in the mast will take some of the fullness out of the luff of the sail and automatically flatten the sail in strong winds as, broadly speaking, the faster the wind the flatter the sail needs to be set.

In Nelson's time masts were solid tree-trunks and the larger ones were made up of many pieces of timber bound together by iron bands; so they were strong and sturdy by themselves. Indeed, they had to be, because there was no wire rigging in those days—it was all made from vegetable fibre which slackened in dry weather and tightened in wet. Many people today, quite good seamen amongst them, still believe in slack rigging. Good helmsmen often have fallacies like this and win races in spite of them; if they only had their rigging set taut and true they would win that much more easily. It is often the ability of a man as a helmsman and seaman that blinds him and others to defects in the rigging and the setting of his sails.

Today almost all of our masts are light, hollow, wooden spars, and as any tube that bends collapses immediately we must see to it that the rigging of wire is set taut enough to eliminate all the bend possible. The wire rigging is there for that purpose, and because there is little or no stretch in it we can set it exactly as it should be: knowing that once it has been stretched and has settled down it will stand like that throughout the months to come. It stands to reason that if the rigging is slack the mast will fall out of the boat to leeward until the rigging becomes tight enough to take its load; so we might as well put the load that it must bear into the rigging when the boat is launched. In this way the mast will be held in place from the very beginning.

A further point to bear in mind is that, no matter what boat you go on, you can catch hold of the lee rigging and swing it round and round as you would a skipping-rope. This slackness is caused by many things. When the boat is on the quay she is sitting on her ballast keel which is pushing the mast upwards, but directly the boat is launched this ballast keel is suspended from the boat and tends to sink. The boat is now supported by her bilges; so her sides are being lifted up and the centre, where the mast is stepped, is being sunk deeper into the water, resulting in an immediate slackening of the shrouds. When we hoist sail and start putting the loads into our mast, it becomes a strut under compression, irrespective of the material it is made of and shortens, just as the cork of a bottle does when you press it between your finger and thumb. There is also the pull of the shrouds on the weather side stretching the topsides upward, while on the lee side there is a terrific pressure on the lee bilge pushing that side upwards. As well as this there is the mainsheet pulling up from the after end of the boat trying to lift it up, the forestay trying to lift up the boat at the bow, while the mast itself is trying to press the boat down in the centre. So everything tends to slacken the rigging and most people sail with it too slack.

I always see that the forestay and the two main shrouds are bar taut. The lower and also the upper shrouds should be a little slacker, for when sailing it is the jib stay and the main shroud

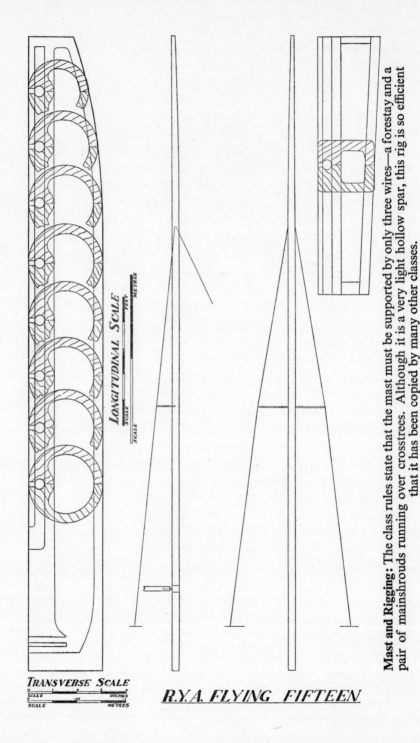

LONGITUDINAL SCALE

SCALE — FEET

SCALE — METRES

TRANSVERSE SCALE

SCALE — INCHES

SCALE .05 — METRES

R.Y.A. FLYING FIFTEEN

Mast and Rigging: The class rules state that the mast must be supported by only three wires—a forestay and a pair of mainshrouds running over crosstrees. Although it is a very light hollow spar, this rig is so efficient that it has been copied by many other classes.

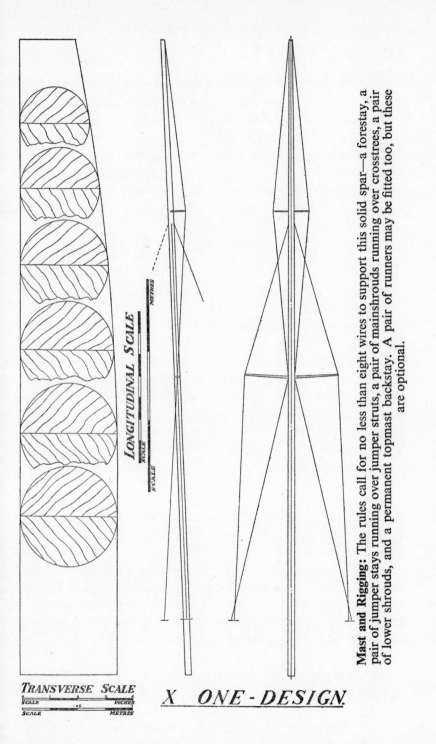

LONGITUDINAL SCALE

SCALE METRES

SCALE

SCALE

TRANSVERSE SCALE

SCALE · 05 INCHES

SCALE METRES

X ONE-DESIGN.

Mast and Rigging: The rules call for no less than eight wires to support this solid spar—a forestay, a pair of jumper stays running over jumper struts, a pair of mainshrouds running over crosstrees, a pair of lower shrouds, and a permanent topmast backstay. A pair of runners may be fitted too, but these are optional.

attached at this point that we need to keep firm and secure. The rest of the rigging takes less load, so may very well be a little easier —especially the lower shrouds, which are so short that there is little or no give in them. Thus, when the boat is sailing in a smart breeze, there is almost equal tension on all shrouds and the mast is dead straight athwartships and fore and aft in a moderate breeze. When we haul in our mainsheet hard in a strong breeze, the top of the mast tends to bow aft, and below the jib halyard to bow forward. This flattens our mainsail, which is what we want.

Having felt all our shrouds for tautness and pulled our mainsail out along the foot of the boom until all the wrinkles have disappeared, we are ready to launch. All we do is just heave away on the winch handle to lift our boat a few inches clear of the quay, swing her round and drop her into the water on the brake. Then we unhook our sling wire, swing the crane back over the quay, and we are afloat and free.

We now haul our mainsail up until all the wrinkles have only just disappeared from the luff and the weight is equal on the luff rope and on the luff of the sail. Then we haul up our jib so that there is exactly the same weight on the luff of the jib as there is on the forestay. Now we take a good look at the lead of the jib-sheet to see that this is in the right place. If it is too far forward the leech will be tight and throw the wind back into the mainsail, but if it is too far aft the leech will be too slack and the jib will shake the whole boat so that we cannot tell whether we are sailing on or off the wind.

The rig on a Flying Fifteen is simplicity itself. There is only one forestay and two shrouds to adjust and as these automatically tighten each other there is very little to worry about except to ensure that both shrouds are of the same length, otherwise the mast will be leaning out to port or starboard when set. As there are only these three wires holding it, it naturally follows that as we pull in tight on our mainsheet we bow the top of the mast and this bows the mast forward halfway between the jib halyard and the deck. So we can flatten our mainsail or give it fullness by the amount we harden in on the mainsheet. As we pull our sails in tighter in strong winds than in light we have a fairly full mainsail in light airs and a flat one in a breeze of wind with this rig.

The X boat, although still having a simple rigging plan, has eight members to her standing rigging as against the three of the Flying Fifteen; so there is more to think about and more skill is required in adjusting it.

First of all, the forestay and the main shrouds should be set taut so that the mast has little or no movement at the jib halyard. The lower shrouds should be set a little slacker, though still fairly taut, so that when the mast goes out of the boat to leeward—no matter how little—it is straight. To support the masthead there are two jumper stays going over jumper struts which make an angle of 100°. These run from the topmast head to the lower shroud band and, ideally, these jumper stays should lead down to within reach of the deck where their rigging screws can be adjusted; for in light weathers these need to be fairly tight, while in a breeze of wind it is just as well to ease them off and let the masthead bow to flatten the sail. From the topmast head to the stern is the topmast backstay, and although some people slacken this off when running I cannot see that this does any good, as it does not increase the sail area by as much as half a square inch.

These X one-designs can carry a runner from the jib halyard to the deck, the same distance abaft the mast as the forestay is forward of it, but it is an added complication and the mast stands quite well without it. If these are added it means that she has ten parts to her standing rigging; more than three times as many as a little Flying Fifteen.

Now we hoist our sails and away we go. The first thing to do is to put your eye on the aft side of the mast and look up it when the sails are full of wind and the boat well heeled. The mast should then be in a straight line athwartships and either straight in the fore and aft direction or with the mast head bowed aft and the belly of the mast bowed forward in an easy and fair curve, according to the weight of wind and the weight on the mainsheet. It is surprising how few people look up their masts when there is a hatful of wind; much can be learnt by doing this and it is the only way I know of ensuring that all the rigging is adjusted to a nicety. And remember that the rigging has to be correct not on the moorings or on the shore, but when you are sailing in a light or heavy breeze.

G

I am fortunate in that, living at Cowes, I have been great friends with three generations of the Ratsey and Lapthorn family of Cowes, Gosport and New York, who have made sails since 1790. Having sailed thousands of miles with them and having gone into their lofts almost every working day for some thirty years I have learnt a great deal from their knowledge of sails. The sails are the engine of a boat and too much care cannot be given to them. When we have a new car we run the engine in quietly and gently until all of its parts have settled down in peace and harmony with each other; then we start to turn up the wick and let the car go along at its maximum speed. This is equally true of sails: they should be sailed gently and kindly until they are stretched and settled down to the mast and boom. Only after they have been broken in can we use them in any weather. I do not believe I can do better than record some of Ratsey's and Lapthorn's thoughts on the bending, stretching and care of sails, together with my own:

Stretching a New Cotton Sail

Choose a fine sunny day with a light breeze of about 10 m.p.h. Never sail with a new sail in blowing weather or if it is foggy, raining or at all damp. Never reef a new sail; until it has been fully stretched a sail cannot endure reefing. But you should not go out with a new sail when there is no wind at all.

Pull the sail out on the boom end until all the wrinkles in the foot just disappear and no more. Luff and foot ropes vary, but it is your sail you are breaking in and caring for so you must haul it out until the wrinkles in it are gone. If it is rope bound and this rope is tight you must exert greater strength to haul it out than you would on one where the rope was slack. Now hoist away on your halyard, set the luff until it is just taut, and you are ready to sail.

The leech of a sail is seldom roped except in large and cruising vessels. It is generally cut with a rounded edge or roach as this is unmeasured sail area and is free. As the sail stretches this roach disappears or diminishes. There are batten pockets sewn in this leech at equal intervals and you must never hoist a sail without inserting all of its battens. If they are not used the roach will not hold itself flat, and the weight of the boom will stretch the sail in a straight line from the top to the outer end of the main boom, but with the battens in place this strain will spread evenly over all the sail. The unroped leech of the sail will stretch practically all that it is ever going to stretch the first time the sail is set and used. This is the reason why you pull the sail out until the wrinkles have disappeared on the foot and luff; otherwise the boom will droop, putting extra strain on the leech and stretching it unduly.

When hoisting the sail the weight of the boom must be carried either on a topping lift or, in a small boat, in your hand. You must not allow the sail to take any weight of the boom until the halyard and luff are set taut and the strain is equal all over the sail.

Once the mainsail is set, leave the mooring immediately, otherwise your boat will lie head to wind, causing the sail to shake and rattle. It is going to get more shaking than ever it needs throughout its life and this shaking gradually destroys the cloth by causing all the minute threads and fibres of cotton to chafe against each other. So, directly your mainsail is set, drop your moorings and sail about, reaching to and fro with the wind abeam; not hard on the wind as the leech area stretches first. Soon little wrinkles will appear on the luff and foot, evidence that they have started to stretch, and while this is happening you must haul out on the boom and haul up on the halyard continually. But although the luff and foot must be kept taut, do not put undue strains on them, and only pull out until the wrinkles have disappeared. In large vessels you must, of course, lower the mainsail until it is quiet enough to be stretched out along its boom.

A sail needs five or six hours' quiet, gentle stretching in warm, sunny weather with a wind of about 10 m.p.h. Some take longer, but this is the minimum time.

If your jib has a wire luff there is no need to worry about luff stretch—this has already been done by the sailmaker. You set the wire luff of the jib to the same tension as the forestay.

Synthetic Sails

These are generally made of Terylene, a British invention known in America as Dacron, which differs from cotton in the following ways:

Very small absorption of water.

Does not shrink when wet.

At least twice as strong as cotton.

Good resistance to mildew.

Stows in a small space.

Smooth surface.

Less stretch than cotton.

(Sunlight affects it to the same degree as cotton.)

You do not have to worry about this material as much as cotton in wet weather, salt spray or dampness of any kind. Then there is Nylon, which is more elastic and although good for spinnakers, is not good for standing sails such as the mainsail or jib. The strength of Nylon is also seriously affected by a great deal of sunlight, so it should not be left exposed to the sun's rays for long periods.

Stretching a Terylene Sail

This calls for the same procedure as with a cotton sail but takes much less time, as it does not matter if it is raining or snowing, and only two hours' sailing in a reasonable wind will see the sail fully stretched and ready to race or cruise. However, once again, it is always better to be over-cautious than daring.

The Flow in Sails

Almost all who sail know that the most effective form for the sail itself is one which, broadly speaking, is a parabolic curve: like the top of a bird's wing. This has the greatest flow forward, flattening out to a straight line at the leech, and is the ideal to aim for in all your sails.

Spars

Nearly all spars are tapered on the opposite side to which the sail is attached: so you should look not only up the aft side of the mast to see that it is straight and that the luff is snug in at the aft side at the tack (unless it has been cut specially to come back to the gooseneck) but along your boom as well. When you are sailing along in a smart breeze you go to the fore end of the boom, put your eye as close to the gooseneck as you can, and sight along the top of the boom. It should be straight, but it is surprising how often a boom bends and how much, all of which has an effect on the sail. If the boom bends up in its centre it throws fullness into the sail; if it curves down in the centre it will flatten the sail. On all boats I spend a great deal of time sighting up the after side of the mast and sighting along the top edge of the boom. Then I go out on the stemhead or the bowsprit and sight up the forestay to see how much sag there is in that. We must know what our spars and stays are like in a breeze of wind as well as in light weather, for only then can we tell if the fault of the bad-setting sail lies in the sail itself or in the spars and tension of the rigging.

Battens

Today there are many plastic battens, and these cannot be tapered on their inner ends; for this reason I prefer hickory battens. They are lighter and stronger than plastic; float if they drop overboard; can be tapered so that their inner ends are pliable; and will easily take up the curve required by the sail.

Battens must be an inch or more shorter than the pockets into which they have to fit. The sail is like a piece of elastic which, as it stretches, gets narrower. As the sail is hoisted the luff and leech are stretched and narrowed—and this means shorter pockets. If the battens are too long they make a great poke in the mainsail, and may also chafe a hole through the inner end of the batten pocket and even through the sail itself.

In light-weather sailing, when you are putting more curve into your sail, you need a more flexible top batten than usual, the rest of the sail being so wide that it is still flat on its back edge even in a light breeze.

All hickory battens should be protected by two or more coats of varnish, otherwise, being wood, they will warp and twist when wet.

Headsails

Headsails usually have wire luffs and are loose-footed, so they must be set up taut the first time—the luff having already been stretched out on the wire by the sailmaker. But, here again, it is advisable to use them in the beginning as you do a mainsail—in a 10 or 12 m.p.h. wind and warm sunshine. Then the sail can develop and stretch itself naturally and pleasantly, which makes for a well-setting sail with a long life.

Most headsails today are cut with a mitre seam which bisects the angle at the clew. Generally the jib fairlead should be a continuation of this mitre line dropped at an angle of 5° from the clew. This is only a rough guide for the position of the fairlead, which can only be finally placed on trial, as it is not only the jib itself we think of but the mainsail too. The mainsail up and down takes on a curve, as does the leech of the jib; this should marry up and run as parallel as possible with the up and down curve of the mainsail at this point. If the jib fairlead is too far forward it will flatten the curve to leeward of the leech, which in turn will throw back the wind on to the mainsail and prevent the mainsail working to its full extent. On the other hand, if the jib fairlead is too far aft, the leech of the jib will fall off and sag away to leeward in its centre, and lose a great deal of the effectiveness from the most powerful part of this sail.

Overlapping jibs—and, in fact, most jibs—should be sheeted well out from the centre-line. The smaller the jib the finer the angle required from the centre-line, and the faster the boat the finer the angle—the average being about 12°. All of this points to the importance of having a taut and straight forestay with no sag in it; for if the headstay sags, it lets the luff of the sail out to leeward, and this cannot go very far without preventing any angle at all from being made with the centre-line. When this happens the headsail has no drive forward; it only presses the boat over sideways and so becomes a punishing sail with no drive.

Spinnakers

Of late years spinnaker booms have been getting higher and higher. In the old days you seldom saw a spinnaker boom set high enough on the mast at its inner end, but there is now a tendency to lift it so far up that a great deal of the spinnaker's frontal area is lost and a staysail has to be set underneath to fill in the gap caused by the high-flying sail.

Reefing

We reef only about once in thirty days, cruising or racing; generally when race committees see enough wind to reef, they get cold feet and cancel the regatta, which destroys the day's sport and tends to make us into a lot of weak-kneed, fair-weather sailors. So, time and time again, we see racing boats—which normally set their sails perfectly—go out with a badly taken-in reef, and this can easily ruin a sail for all time.

If you have tie-down reefs, lash the tack earring down tight on the boom in line with the track of the boom, then pull out the reef earring on the leech of the sail until it is taut along the row of reef points or lacing eyes and also make this fast. Then neither, the tack nor the clew earring can work in towards each other when the strain comes on the sail.

Some sails have reef points but others have eyelets and a lacing. I prefer the lacing because, rove through and hauled down, it will ease itself so that the strain is equal on all the eyelets, in exactly the same way that a boot-lace does. If, however, you have reef points and you tie each one down individually, see that they all bear an equal strain and are all equally taut; for if one is tighter than the others, it can tear the sail, and in blowing weather this can lead to a great deal of trouble. Also, when shaking out the reef, untie all the reef points first and make certain that every reef point is really untied. If one is left tied down, when you hoist away on the sail you will tear it.

The sail is, of course, carefully and neatly rolled in before the points or lacing are made fast, and this must be round the foot of the sail and not round the boom. If it is round the boom the rope will chafe and cut through the boom, and will itself be chafed. When shaking out a reef underway, the reef points must be eased away from the centre of the sail first, then worked towards the two ends. Once this has been slacked or undone, let go the tack reef earring first, then the clew, and hoist away, making sure that the topping lift is taking the weight of the boom. Otherwise the boom will come crashing down on deck or into the cockpit. Even if you do not shake out the reef before you arrive at the moorings you must do this on arrival. The sail is bound to be damp, and leaving it reefed will not only cause mildew but also put an undue stretch in the sail along the row of reef points.

Wet Weather (Cotton and Flax Sails)

With cotton or flax sails, when it starts to rain or when a fog or mist comes on, the canvas will begin to shrink before the rope, so, unless the halyards and outhauls are slacked up bit by bit, the sail cannot shrink evenly and naturally. When you have finished sailing and are on the moorings or at anchor, you should ease away on all outhauls; then, if there is dampness through the night or if damp weather sets in, the sails will shrink naturally and not come to any harm.

Mildew and Rot

Never furl up a wet sail, but bundle it up loosely so that the air can get to it, thus guarding against mildew and rot.

When drying sails we must remember that the corners—which are reinforced by many thicknesses of canvas—and the roping of the sails take a lot longer to dry than the single thickness of the canvas; so we must allow more time for these thicker parts. Although Terylene is not affected by mildew it will still be all the better for careful treatment.

Sail Covers

Sail covers keep out the worst of the wet and keep the sails clean; but we must remember that damp will find its way down past the mast and inside the best cover ever made and damp air will swirl up underneath the cover. So after a rainy spell remove the sail covers as soon as possible to let in dry air and sunlight and prevent mildew and rot from setting in. Never cover up a sail which is wet or even damp, for the first little ray of sunlight will cause steaming and rot.

Salt Spray (Cotton and Flax Sails)

Small boats and yachts, sometimes even large ones, time and time again get their sails soaked with spray, so even when dry, sails of light material crackle like a piece of paper when handled in dry weather. In damp and foggy weather the salt absorbs the moisture in the air and the sail is immediately wet: the part that has the salt on it will shrink and the rest will remain as it is so you will have a badly-setting sail. The remedy is to rinse them with fresh water; small ones can be put in the bath and the larger ones hosed down on a quay or lawn.

Laying Up Winter Storage and Fitting Out

What is true of a small vessel is largely true of all, so we will look in detail at the laying up, winter storage, fitting out, preparing for a race and settling down afterwards, of a Flying Fifteen (the smallest and least costly of keel yachts); also the care of her spars, rigging, sails, sheets and gear.

When laying up for the winter we must remember that the sun is now 1,500 miles south of the Line, and shines through the earth's atmosphere at such an angle that its power is diminished; and the days are short and the nights long. Therefore, our boat is going to endure a dreat deal of damp, cold atmosphere which will sap away the strength of its protective paints and varnishes. A small electric bulb which can be switched on inside for the damp days will help to keep the hull and its finishes healthy and happy through the winter.

The first job is to remove the battens and get the sails off their spars and stays; then they must be washed clean and dried, the battens removed, and the sails stored in a clean dry place, free from mice and rats and with a current of dry air. But, if you can arrange it, send them to their maker. All sailmakers are deeply interested in the sails they have made, so it is far better to let him wash and store them for the winter and do any repairs that he can, in the autumn. Write the list of sails, their repairs, and his instructions clearly and in duplicate, so there are no doubts in his or your mind. "Wash, dry, do all repairs required, air and store for winter and deliver to me on May 1st." Then, when spring comes and everyone is clamouring for sails, yours will have been overhauled and repaired, and will be in perfect order; and you can start the season off on the right foot.

Now you unreeve all sheets and running rigging, which are of rope; at the same time looking to see what should be renewed and what "end for ended"—this is, changing the ends and so doubling the life of a rope.

Next you take your spars, mainboom, spinnaker boom, boat

hook, and sweeps or paddle ashore, wash off the salt, rub down with wet or dry glass-paper or cuttle fish, then paint or varnish in the autumn or late summer sun. This will protect them through the winter and thus save double the time in the spring.

Now lift out the mast, take off the rigging and examine and renew as required. Wipe all wire rigging and fittings with a lanoline (grease of sheep's wool) covered rag, to preserve it for the winter. Repeat the treatment given to the other spars. All of them should now be stored on a rack or hung from the roof so that they keep straight and true throughout the six or so months during which the ship is laid up.

Most small boats' masts and booms today have a groove into which the luff and foot slide; this saves weight, windage, the cost of a track and screws, and is aerodynamically correct as no wind can escape and upset the flow of air on luff and foot. Both the mast and boom should be stored groove downwards; then, if by chance any water drives in it cannot remain there and harm the groove, neither can dust settle and cake in it. This is also true of metal tracks; and both they and the groove need padding under their winter supports to ensure that no harm come to them.

Next you haul or lift the vessel out of the water, and as she comes up wash her down well with fresh water, inside and out, to remove all the salt of the sea. After she has dried out, paint or varnish any thin or bare places. Paints, enamels and varnishes protect our vessels as well as beautifying them, just as clothes protect as well as adorn us, and defend us from the burning sun and the chilling breeze. As we would not dream of enduring the cold and damp of winter without the protection of clothing, neither should we allow our vessels and their spars and gear to do so without their protective paints and varnishes.

We get many kind days until early January and when I lived at Puckester Cove, on the southern point of the Island, I often enjoyed breakfast out of doors in the early morning sun until January 2nd or 3rd. Then the cold weather would set in until the end of March, showing the truth of that old couplet:

> *As the day lengthens*
> *So the cold strengthens.*

Therefore, if you live in the South of England you can, as we often did, keep your vessel out until the middle of December, and enjoy many a lovely week-end in spite of the short days and long nights. When I was younger, my 20-ton schooner was seldom laid up, as a little gang of us used to go duck shooting at the week-ends off the mud flats of Keyhaven and Lymington. I used a four-bore from the shoulder and she would bring down wildfowl at ninety to a hundred yards.

The winter is divided into five little winters, with lots of warm sunny spells in between, and the last of all is blackthorn winter, when the white flower of the blackthorn gladdens all the hedge-rows and woods. By then the days are long and the sun is strong, as it has now recrossed the line and is some 2,500 miles nearer to us, and the innocents, believing we have summer with us, leave off clothes. Then the piercing and penetratingly cold, north-east wind of blackthorn winter searches them out and they fall sick. After the blackthorn the whitethorn, or May, comes into blossom. If it is an early summer this comes out early in May, but often does not blossom until the middle or very end of the month; hence the old rhyme is of the flower, not the month:

Ne'er cast a clout
Till May be out.

All this must be borne in mind when painting, varnishing or putting on enamels. You should never rub down and leave the wood exposed in winter, for this lets in the damp; and in summer you should never let bare wood endure the heat of the sun either. So plan to rub down in the morning and coat this up before 2.00 p.m., for in winter there are one or two hours for the surface to harden before night falls, as there is no dryness in the night air.

The final coats must go on in one, without a join. By now the days are long and the sun has some power, and all the under-coats are keeping out the weather, so you can rub down and pre-pare for the final coat. Apply it at 11.00 a.m. and finish before 2.00 p.m. The warmer the day the better the result. If you are going to antifoul your ship's bottom, you must remember that antifouling does not protect or preserve the vessel, be it wood or iron. It is a gas paint to kill weeds and any marine life that attacks it. This paint, unlike the others, should be put on at the last possible moment, so that its gases remain sealed by the water on launching, until they are released by the marine growth attacking the bottom.

So, by starting to prepare for our spring launching from the day we haul out in the autumn, all is done quietly and steadily and makes a winter amusement. There is no sudden jerk; it is like ploughing a large field with horses—slowly but surely the work is done.

With our ship ready and gleaming in the spring sunshine, reflecting all about her in her decks, topsides, boot top, and bottom, we ship masts, spars, gear and sails and we are ready for sea in no time. The mast stepped, there is the standing rigging to adjust. We must set this taut, otherwise the mast will bend out of the boat before the wire shrouds can start to do their job of supporting the mast. If you have more than one set of shrouds, each side of these should be set bar taut at the top and, as they come down the mast, not quite so tight, the lower shrouds being just taut without a strain on them. The reason for this is that the main shrouds at the jib halyard height are taking the greatest strain, so most of this load should be put in them while the boat is at rest. Then those beneath should be adjusted so that when the vessel is sailing hard her mast is straight. You can easily see this by looking up the track at the aft side of the mast when sailing in a brisk breeze.

Another point to remember is that there is a certain amount of stretch and give, however small, in wire rigging, and the longer the wire the greater the stretch. Running rigging should also be of wire from the head of the sail to its belaying point, for rope stretches continually and with rope halyards we are forever setting up our sails.

Now take a look over the mainsheet to see that all is well, and look very carefully at the jibsheet for position of the lead. If this is too far forward, it will pull the leech down too tightly and so throw wind back into the mainsail; if it is too far aft, it will give a flat foot and loosen the leech. The correct position for the jibsheet lead is one of the most important points of a vessel. The jib is the foremost sail and, cutting into clean, undisturbed wind, deflects it; so much depends on the correct trimming of this sail that too much importance cannot be placed in its shape, cut and set, all of which can be ruined by the jibsheet lead being wrongly placed.

You next take a look at your spinnaker and all its gear. In small vessels, including 12-metres this is always set flying, being controlled only on its three corners by halyard, guy and sheet. It is a difficult sail to set as it must be done perfectly; so ensure that all is in readiness for the five vital seconds of its setting during a race. It is so much more easily done before getting underway, as a boat lying still brings calmer thoughts than one plunging through the waters.

Now see that the buoyant apparatus for the boat and for all on board is correct, pumps and bailers in order, and you are ready to launch.

I am fortunate; the sea is around three sides of my house, and there is a crane on the quay which lifts the little boats I have in and out of the water like a fish on a rod and line. One man on the crane, the others to steady the boat, and in 45 seconds a boat can be afloat, unhooked and away, and we can sail yet another summer sea to our heart's content.

V

Racing

HAVING learnt to sail and handle a boat, the earlier you can start racing the better. Once you race, every fault is pointed out in the way the other boats sail away from you, and when you do anything well this too is revealed as you start sailing away from the rest of the fleet. Cruising men, on the other hand, try to avoid everything. They give other craft a good wide berth and so do not learn to handle their boats in an exact manner. When we drive a car along our roads we miss other cars by inches all day long. In a day's drive we learn to steer and handle a car with great exactness; so it is with sailing a race. When we are on the port tack we have to give way to starboard tack boats; if we touch the mark on rounding we are disqualified and have to retire, yet, if we leave the mark 10 yards wide we have to sail this 10 yards back again. As we are rounding marks and buoys throughout the race—possibly rounding ten different marks—if we give each mark a 10-yard berth and have to sail the same 10 yards back again we have made the race 200 yards longer for ourselves. We can never win a race doing this. We also learn to judge with great exactness the speed and the ability of our boat.

In the five minutes before the race starts we are manœuvring our vessel in close proximity to the others under the watchful eye of a sailing committee. Once the five minutes signal is made we come under the racing rules and can be disqualified for any breach of the rules. When, finally, the starting-gun has gone we attempt to cross the line in the best position with full way on, within a second or so of gun-fire. Because we are attempting to get the utmost out of our boat we watch every cloud, every squall, and every shift of wind; for races that take hours to sail are often won by seconds. Time and time again only 30 seconds divide the first six boats.

Therefore, though a man may take up sailing in order to go cruising, it will be well for him to race for a season early in his sailing career. It will teach him perfection in the handling and sailing of his craft; which will stand him in good stead when he goes cruising. It is frequently the cruising man who has raced who makes his harbour without any trouble; whereas a man who has only cruised goes about things in a much more slovenly manner, for he has not the exactness and the skill found in racing men.

Through my life I have taken part in almost every sport. When you are boxing you are either giving punishment to another man, receiving it yourself, or by skilful footwork avoiding it; when you are cross-country running you have all the physical joy of running a little faster than the other man; he does not touch or harm you—you are just running, it is a pure test of physical strength and so brings great joy into your heart. So it is in sailing a race; you sail your boat without touching another and derive a great deal of pure joy from the boat's speed through the water with her sheets trimmed to perfection and the steersman interfering with her as little as possible. Generally speaking, a man derives his greatest pleasure from his day's work; he is either sad that it has not been done to his satisfaction, or full of joy because it has been done well that day. We get all this joy endeavouring to sail to perfection throughout a race.

Nothing is perfect in this world and we can never sail a perfect race; but if we make only one mistake—providing it is not a fatal one—we should come in first. Two mistakes make us second, and three mistakes bring us into third place.

As we race our sailing vessel we should try to sail clear of the fleet, as then we are not interfered with by other boats and only then can we give all our thoughts and energies to our own—to the trim of her sheets, the flaws of wind, the squalls and lulls, the different run in the tide and the hundred and one little things around us all day long. Whenever I race, I try to get off on my own, away from the fleet where I have only my own vessel, her sails, rig and crew, to consider.

A great many people try to win races by spoiling tactics such as interfering with another vessel's wind. These people do not aim at sailing their own boat fast, but try to stop other people sailing theirs fast. Of course, when in close company with another vessel, we at all times possible try to sit on her wind, keeping our own free. But generally a race is more fun clear of the fleet where you can devote all your energies and thought to your own boat, which is quite enough to occupy any brain.

There are many rules which must be obeyed and if you break any you are out of the race. In most sports there are referees or umpires, but in yacht racing you are your own judge. Because of this you must pay very strict attention to the rules, for although you can now break them unobserved through being clear of the fleet, you cannot escape from your own conscience and you would have no satisfaction in winning a race knowing you had broken a rule in order to do so.

Sailing races have been arranged for hundreds of years and they still take place without a referee or umpire. This tells us of the honesty of sailing people : and long may it continue.

All racing in this country is under the control of the Royal Yachting Association and international racing under the International Yacht Racing Union which has from the very beginning met in London under the wing of our Royal Yachting Association. This shows that all countries look upon Britain as being fair-minded, and also that the R.Y.A. is a very important body, so all taking part in yacht racing should join it and give it added strength and encouragement by their membership. As well as this, you should join the club under whose burgee you propose to do your greatest amount of racing.

Before we can race we must study the R.Y.A. racing rules. Until 1959 these were all based on the international rule of the road at sea. Then, in 1959, an American set of rules came in ; and now the racing man has to know two sets of rules. Whenever he meets a vessel—trading or cruising, or a racing vessel before or after her race and not actually racing—he has to conform to the Rule of the Road at Sea to avoid an accident and the risk of paying a damage claim. And he must also know the new Racing Rules. When racing in 1959 in the Solent, we came upon twelve boats sailing exactly the same course, and we had to give way to only one of them, because this racer had taken down her racing flag: to my mind a most stupid situation.

The Racing Rules demand that ten minutes before the start a warning gun should be fired to draw attention to the class flag that has been broken out at that moment. Remember it is the flag that is the signal—the gun or horn or other noise is only to draw attention to the flag. Five minutes later, exactly to the second, the Blue Peter is broken out and the second gun fired—the five-minute signal. Now all in this class come under the Rules of Racing, for although there is no proper course, as all the boats are darting and weaving to and fro like swallows in an endeavour to make the best start, the rules must be obeyed. Five minutes later the Blue Peter and the class flag are hauled down. This is the signal to start, and attention is drawn to it by the starting-gun. As we all know guns sometimes misfire, and that is why it is most important to look at the flags, for these are the signals.

Away we go on our course. For five minutes we have manœuvred hoping that we should start across the line in the best position—sometimes to windward, sometimes to leeward, sometimes in the middle of the line—and cross it with full way on so that we pull right ahead of the fleet. But as all the rest are bent on doing the same thing it is extremely difficult and needs very exact timing and a great understanding of our boat and of the virtues and flaws in our crew. For if we have a bad crew we have to make our start with a minimum of turns and a minimum of action on the crew's part.

So off we go, round the course full of hope.

Hard-Weather Racing

When racing in strong breezes and heavy winds we must always carry more sail to windward than our boat can really stand. There are many reasons for this. Although she is overcanvassed in the squalls, sometimes wallowing, and so slowed up, there are many lulls between them and in these she will be travelling at her top speed. And if we are skilful we can also keep our vessel on her feet and travelling at her top speed through the squalls, which is where we gain on those who do not know. Readers will remember what I said in Chapter III about sailing to windward, and of course this applies to racing as well. Here where we must use every ounce of wind pressure to keep up our speed, it is particularly important

H

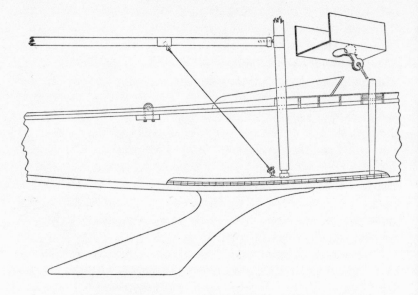

KICKING STRAP F.F.

I invented the kicking-strap to work off the wind; its purpose is to keep the boom down so that the mainsail swings off in one plane when the mainsheet is slacked away. This means that when it is eased for reaching with a tackle or winch—as it often is—its whole value is lost. This illustration is of the strong dead length wire rubber-covered kicking-strap used on Prince Philip's Flying Fifteen *Coweslip* for more than ten years.

to be able to adjust our sails quickly and easily so that we do not lose way. When I discovered that I had to ease a great deal of sheet off to get any relief from the pressure of wind, my mind travelled back over the years to a cruise to the Bermudas where 14-ft. dinghies with a crew of six carry as much sail as our 6 metres —450 sq. ft.—in a brisk breeze. The reason they could carry all this sail was that their mainbooms were well up on the mast high above the tack which meant that the outer end of the mainsail could not lift, and that the whole sail swung out in one plane when the sheet was eased like a door on its hinges. So a great deal of pressure was eased out of it swiftly with the minimum of sheet, and as well as this there was much less strain on the mainsheet. We tried such a boom but with the small mainsails allowed by our rules we could not afford the loss of efficiency caused by this boom. When it was to windward of the loose-footed mainsail it had its deepest flow at half its width, instead of at one-third from the luff, which it has when the flow is controlled by the curved mainsail foot attached to the boom. When the boom was to leeward, the mainsail at this point was absolutely flat with no flow at all. Then we tried a split-wishbone boom curved on either side of the sail; but although this was better the flow was still too far aft as it always is in a loose-footed mainsail. Finally I invented the wire kicking-strap, which was attached to the boom and mast so that it made an angle of 45° to the mast and this, by preventing the boom from lifting, gave us instant relief on easing away the least bit of the mainsheet. It put a great deal of strain on the mainboom, but this short spar could stand it: and so the kicking-strap was invented and has been a boon to sailing men ever since.

Another great help was a wide mainsheet horse, as this pulled the outer end of the mainboom down to the desired angle and eliminated a great twist from the sail. With the final lead of the mainsheet led from the centre of the boom down on deck it acted in a smaller way as an extra kicking-strap. So these things enabled us to carry more sail than we had carried to windward before.

In this way we carried the extra sail that these V-sectioned boats needed to lift them out and set them planing over the surface of the sea, and the newly-developed seagoing planing hull caused me to develop a new technique of sailing—that of playing the mainsheet in and out as you do a heavy game fish on a light line. And this, in turn, put more zip and zest into sailing so that today's standard of sailing is far above that of thirty years ago.

Light-Weather Racing

When there is hardly a wag of wind you put up your ghosting sails—the lightest ones you have, though not always the largest. For though the material in the sails is light, once it exceeds a certain area the bulk is so great that the light air cannot move it. Now, with your ghosting headsail up, you start the difficult job of making your boat travel fast with hardly a breath of wind.

The great thing to do is to keep the boat moving through the water. Never attempt to sail really tight up on the wind but keep her footing as fast as possible, so that you will often be sailing, not close-hauled, but one point free of this, covering a greater distance, searching for more wind. When you go on to the other tack do this as quietly and slowly as you can, as it is surprising how long a boat will carry her way with gentle use of the rudder. In the old days the big five—*Britannia, Westward, White Heather, Lulworth* and *Shamrock*—in light airs and the smooth water that went with them, were allowed to shoot dead into the eye of the wind when going through it, for almost a quarter of a mile before they were thrown over on the other tack; for once these long, shapely vessels had gathered energy they maintained it a long while under these conditions.

You will remember how I told in Chapter III of the way we won a race in *Fresh Breeze* on a very calm day. As we did then, so in light airs move quietly yet firmly about the decks, handle all sails as peacefully as possible, and use the minimum amount of helm—and so build up and keep the energy of your vessel as high and long as possible.

Now we can see that though in easy weather conditions with a moderate breeze of 15 m.p.h. the new entry is on an equal footing with the experienced seaman, this is not so in the difficult conditions brought about by light airs or strong winds. It is in these extremes of weather that the wisdom gained by years of sailing and seamanship tells. To sail without wind is as difficult as it is to skate without ice, yet the expert often seems to sail without wind; so we all should at all times try to understand the ways of wind and sea.

Inland Waters

It is difficult to realise that the inland waterways of Britain are equal to the distance across the Atlantic; there are over three thousand miles of navigable rivers and canals, as well as lakes and other waters, in the British Isles. Because the triumphant and ever-hungry sea is dangerous for the novice, a great many people start their life afloat on the inland waters of this country. These inland waters, although not as dangerous as the sea itself, call for great skill and exact judgment and finesse in boat-handling. I have enjoyed the Norfolk Broads, the Upper Thames, and sailing on that wonderful new reservoir at Pitsford with the Northamptonshire Sailing Club and many other inland waters, and have always admired the great ability of inland-water sailors.

We cannot help admiring the poetry of motion of the racing eights at Henley, and I am fortunate enough to be an honorary member of the Henley Sailing Club with which I have spent many delightful hours. In the old days there were two annual matches between the Henley and the Island Sailing Clubs, one inland and one on the Solent Sea, and from these I learned a great deal.

The difference between a fisherman and an angler is that the fisherman lowers his line out of his boat into the sea and counts his fish by the bucketful or the hundredweights. His skill lies in getting his vessel where the fish are feeding; whereas the angler has not only to select the right part of the river or stream from which to fish, but also to cast his fly in the exact spot so that it alights with all the semblance of an insect on the water. His great joy comes from infinite patience and his own wonderful skill; he does not catch anything like the amount of fish that the sea fisherman gets, but his skill is none the less for it. So it is with sailing: on the sea we can sail hundreds of thousands of miles and on the river tens of miles, but these tens of miles call for the utmost skill and attention to detail.

Today, wherever there is water, whether it is a canal, a gravel pit, lake or river inland, there you will find people sailing; and in many places throughout the winter, too. Over thirty years ago Douglas Heard, who now lives in Ireland, and the other flag officers of the Ranelagh Sailing Club, with myself, started winter sailing programmes over the Boat Race course at Putney; and such is the enthusiasm that they have continued throughout the years and have grown in popularity. So in the heart of London you can have sailing races throughout the whole year. This lead has been followed by a great many other inland clubs for, generally speaking, at sea the greater part of the clubs finish sailing at the end of September and a few continue till Christmas; there is very little sailing at sea for pleasure in the dreadful months of January and February. When March comes, although the weather is still cold and the winds boisterous, the longer days have enticed many sea sailors out, but the inland-watermen have been sailing all winter.

At various open meetings on the sea I have always been struck by the perfect condition of the boats from inland and by their owners' wonderful ability in light-weather sailing. On the Solent, where we have a 4-knot tide, we tend not to be good light-weather sailors for with this 4-knot tide in a calm we can still sail quite fast, because the tide itself gives us a 4-knot breeze. So we can tack to windward with the tide and range to and fro across the Solent. But on arrival at the down-tide mark we have to anchor, as we cannot sail against the tide unless we have quite a breeze. On the Clyde, where the tide is only one knot, they do develop good light-weather sailors. Broadly speaking, because they are practised in this, the people from the Clyde and from inland tend to be our best light-weather sailors, as in these places sailing with hardly a wag of wind can be practised and perfected. I have sailed in many countries and in many places and whenever I go to sail in a new place I look around, certain in my own mind that there are men in every one of these places who are able to sail faster round their own courses than I am. And they always do.

The great thing about sailing is the variety of conditions under which you sail. Hills, houses and trees all deflect and have their particular effect on the wind, and though we all know this, only the man who has sailed a great deal with these local obstructions knows to what extent they effect the wind, as this varies for different wind strengths and directions. In our own homes we can walk about the rooms in the dark and find things easily without a light; and most good men in their own waters have a similar feeling about the wind and the free puffs: they find them, use them and enjoy them; whereas the stranger does not even know that they exist.

So we who sail on the sea can derive a great deal of pleasure and instruction from sailing inland and we should never miss the opportunity of doing so, while those who sail inland can also gain experience from sailing at sea. All experience broadens our knowledge and so adds to our enjoyment of the sport of sailing. Practically the whole of the 3,000 miles of England's rivers and canals are open to vessels not exceeding 46 ft. in length and 7 ft. in beam and an even larger vessel—of 62 ft. by 14 ft.—can make the wonderful voyage across the Pennine Chain from the Humber to the

Mersey. As these inland waterways take us through remote countryside inaccessible by any other means, they are unexpectedly fascinating, for 95% of their mileage is rural and even when we are going through towns we have the fun of seeing them from a new angle. So just as the inland waterman will add to his pleasures by sailing the seas, so will the seaman increase his joy by seeing the rural beauty of our inland waterways.

Cowes Week

The sailing season of 1959 was unusual in that, in the main, easterlies prevailed throughout the entire summer months and westerlies, which should have reigned through July and August, very seldom broke through. And even when they did, they soon lost their hold, as the following observations will show.

Sunday, July 26th, came in as the third day of this easterly wind, and soon strengthened into a brisk breeze of about 18 m.p.h., gusting to about 22. The Flying Fifteen owned by Brigadier Clark, M.P. for Portsmouth, came flying over from Chichester Harbour for Cowes Week, planing merrily most of the way with her spinnaker set. By late afternoon thunderclouds started to build up and in a rain squall the wind shifted from east to south. Then it veered still farther into the south-west, finally backing and settling in the south once again. Next came a thunderstorm with heavy rain, and this cooled off all the earth, as far as we were concerned; for we were only concerned with Britain and the breezes it caused.

The following day, Monday, came in with a smart south-westerly, which freshened as the day grew, and was still strong in the cool of the evening.

By Tuesday, July 28th, the Island Sailing Club Committee, visualising a dreary, uncomfortable day bobbing about in their anchored committee boat, felt so sorry for themselves that they postponed the race for that day. Yet it was only blowing 25 m.p.h. and cruisers were sailing into Cowes from La Belle France across the Channel, and sailing comfortably about the Solent, though reefed. This habit of cancelling races when there is a brave breeze should be discouraged: it takes the robustness out of the sport and tends to debase sailing from a sport into a game by eliminating all zest and risks. Late that day the clouds, which throughout the day

had been marching in triumph high across the sky, became heavier
and lower, and patches of green appeared in the sky, a sure sign of
rain; at 7 o'clock, in the cool of the evening, flurries of rain started.
But after an hour or so blue patches took the place of the green,
and the wind, decreasing in strength at the coming of nightfall—
there is usually much less wind at night than in the day—told us
that once again the south-west monsoon could not break through.

The wind eased through the night and Wednesday came in with
a light northerly air, for the south-west wind, as usual, had veered
through west-north-west to north, a gentle breeze of about 5
m.p.h., with the sun just breaking through its northerly haze. So
once again, the heat stored up in the land repelled the south-west
wind and its clouds, a wonderful thing for the farmers; for
although some of them on the Isle of Wight had harvested their
barley and some their wheat, there was still a great deal standing,
waiting to be cut and gathered in. And ripe wheat, fully grown, is
heavy and gets heavier with rain which, combined with a strong
wind, soon batters it flat. So although the south-west monsoon
makes sailing exciting and fun if you are racing, and heavy work
if you are cruising and going to windward, it brings heavy losses to
farmers. It is as well to think of those ashore when we are afloat.

But even light-weather summers have their days of strong
breezes. In the Dragon trials, one day's race in a wind of 25 m.p.h.
brought damage to 25% of the Dragon fleet. Masts, rigging, halyards, all carried away. This shows the importance of not cancelling races for strong winds, as this encourages boats to lighten their
rigging beyond the safety factor, which is futile anyway, for in
light weather weight aloft makes little difference to a boat and it is
only in strong winds that the heeling effect of weight aloft is really
felt. All the gear should be strong enough to stand up to all the
wind the vessel can endure, and by continually cancelling races in
strong weather committees alter the aspects of boats so that
instead of sturdy little vessels able to endure wind and sea, they
become light-weather playthings.

The following day came in with more wind, and because of the
great havoc wrought in the fleet the previous day this race was postponed for 24 hours and was sailed on a day that started with a light
northerly, 8 or 10 m.p.h. wind.

The Flying Fifteens had five races which counted for the Championship Cup of Cowes Week, from Monday to Friday, and these might be a guide to people racing at Cowes as, although the winds were light, many of the lessons learned by them can be used in any weather; and the tide, like the poor, is with us alway, so must always be taken into account. The tide, though all-important in light airs, loses some of its importance when the wind gets stronger.

Cowes Week, however, does not change.

The Monday of the week is under the burgee of the Royal London Yacht Club. There were 18 starters in a triangular race for the Flying Fifteen Class, and we were in Prince Philip's *Coweslip*. As he was away in Canada I was the steersman and John Foulsham, a young architect, was the crew. We had a light westerly breeze, and it was high water at 11.30 a.m., which was also our starting-time. The ebb, or west-going tide, had been running for an hour and a half and would run westward throughout the race. The wind was west and it was our first race together for a year, so for safety's sake we decided to start on the starboard tack which, though safe, is always a bad thing when going to the westward with a westerly breeze, as the boats inside are not only favoured by the angle of the starting-line but also, as the wind pulls off the land, they are up to windward.

We were tenth round the first buoy and then had to turn 180° and run back against the tide, which was the undoing of many of the boats ahead. They were swept outwards with the tide under their lee bows into a stronger tide, whereas we gybed and kept close to the Island shore, setting our spinnaker without getting out into this stronger tide. By doing this we sailed from tenth into third place, first place being taken by the President of the Flying Fifteen Association, Brigadier Clark, who was running away swiftly with his spinnaker trimmed to perfection. There was another Fifteen outside him also ahead, and as we ran against the tide to the South Bramble Buoy we three gradually pulled away clear of the fleet. We rounded the South Bramble still in third place and, with our spinnaker still set and drawing, we luffed a little for the Ryde West Middle Buoy.

In Cowes Week you have not only your own class to race against and consider but also many other classes, as there are some 400 starters every day. So you have to make a plan that not only involves your own class but also all these others, and I decided right away, from the South Bramble Buoy, to luff out and so clear all the racing Redwings and other classes. Often, by doing this you get a stronger southerly pulling out of the River Medina. Of course the Brigadier luffed out with us and that brought him out clear, and as the other Flying Fifteen also luffed out with us, our three boats sailed along to windward of all the boats ahead, and we came to the Ryde Middle Buoy in this order. Just before arriving we had to capsize our spinnaker. Otherwise we should have obtained an overlap on Brigadier Clark and if this was to windward he could have luffed us the wrong side of the buoy providing he went there, too, and if it was to leeward we should be tucked safely under his lee and he could say snap to us. So we kept in his wake and ran to the buoy behind him.

Now with the ebb tide away it meant that once we rounded this buoy we would be pushed dead to windward towards the finishing-line by the tide; and as the different boats that had rounded ahead of us were well to windward and sitting on our wind, we tacked immediately on rounding to clear our wind. This was the wrong thing to do, because the fourth boat coming round was well astern of us but with his wind clear he could continue on the starboard tack for the Island shore. And pretty soon he had a lead over us as there was a windshift to the south.

Time and time again I have a feeling that I must do this or that thing. In women it is called "intuition", and in men "sixth sense". I often get this feeling at sea and always obey it. I have won many races through doing so and have come out of dangerous situations, too, by taking notice of it. And at this moment, although the boat behind us had passed us through tacking to the south, I obeyed this urge to tack to the north—though it needed some determination, for the other way looked so right. But as we were now in fourth place, any way, there was nothing more to lose; so we stood northwards—the only boat to do so—and soon we were well to the north of all the other racers. Then suddenly, with a swish, the wind shifted to the north and now we were the weather boat, and able to lay the finishing-line comfortably on the starboard tack with the strongest tide in that part of the Solent under us. With a smart north-westerly we sloshed *Coweslip* along; and lo and behold, as we came to the line we were well ahead of the Flying Fifteen fleet and took the first gun and Major Fitz Patrick Robinson's Cup for the Monday of Cowes Week. We had come from fourth to first place through my obeying an instinct, and all in the last three-quarters of a mile of the race when you would have thought that with a fair tide sweeping all the boats down towards the finishing-line we could never have picked up another place.

The Tuesday of Cowes was again the Royal London Yacht Club's Regatta, and again it was a light north-westerly wind. High tide was at 12.11 p.m. and our start at 12.45; so as the west-going tide starts one and a half hours before high water the ebb tide had been running for two hours, and once again we had a westerly-running tide throughout the race. This was a wonderful day, and as it was the Queen Mother's birthday a Royal Salute of 21 guns was fired at noon. This year, instead of saluting from the Squadron they fired it from H.M.S. *Vigo*, which meant a postponement in our starting-time; so that instead of starting at 12.45 p.m. we started at 1.10 p.m.

The start that day was to the eastward and so we were sailing against the tide with a fair wind. As we manœuvred on the line we rolled our jib up and put a half-hitch round it with the jibsheets so that it could be broken out swiftly by pulling on the jibsheets. At the same time we tucked the jib in between the luff of the jib and the forestay to secure it as high as we could reach, so that it would stay there quietly until required.

In these days of nylon spinnakers you have to keep something on your forestay; because if the damp nylon spinnaker wraps round wire it grips as tight as the clothes on those women you see who fill them so well that you think they have been poured into them and somebody forgot to say "when". This meant that we had our jib set to the right tension on its halyard, all ready to be broken out in an instant should we be suddenly luffed and need it, yet leaving us with a clean fore-triangle that let every breath of air into the spinnaker, keeping it quietly pulling to perfection. So we manœuvred for the line with only the mainsail set but with the spinnaker all ready.

It was difficult to decide the best part of the line to start from.

Inshore there was less tide against us but we were farther away from our first mark, as the line stood to the eastward, where the tide against us was stronger, though the wind was stronger too. We started about three parts out on the line, and might have done well if we had not had a boat right on our weather. Every time we came up to him he cut off our wind as it was west-north-west. So we slowed down, and then all the boats to weather took our wind as we crept through Cowes Roads.

In the meantime the boat that had started well to leeward in less wind with less tide, pulled out right ahead, because what little wind he had was clear. We came up to Old Castle Point with all the fleet in a dead straight line abreast, except for this one boat now well out ahead; so the race started afresh from Old Castle Point.

We were now running against the tide, well inshore, everyone of us afraid to go out into the stronger tide to round the Ryde West Middle Buoy, as to go out too soon would have been fatal, for we would swiftly have been swept back to the starting-line and beyond. Suddenly we decided to luff on out across the sterns of the other boats and soon all the fleet came out with us as it was apparent that I had judged the right moment to luff. We rounded the Ryde West Middle Buoy in seventh place, having picked up several places going out. We kept our spinnaker up until we were past this buoy, because of the strength of the tide and the lightness of the air, knowing full well that the tide would sweep us to weather once we were at the buoy. I luffed before the spinnaker was dropped, an unseamanlike manœuvre as it made sail drill an uproar, but sensible during this flurry as while John was struggling, enveloped blindly in the spinnaker and I was moaning and groaning instructions, we jumped past two boats and sailed across for the South Bramble Buoy, now up into fifth place. After rounding this it was a reach across the west-going tide, with well-eased sheets, for the East Gurnard Buoy.

A straight line is the shortest distance between two points and I have gained many places when racing, by steering the shortest course. Few seem to be able to do this, yet it is so simple when you know how. You look at the land or sky behind your mark and keep the mark steady on land or sky; then, although you are not actually steering on the mark itself, your vessel is going straight for it. Prince Philip is a great seaman, and in one race, when our next mark was so far away that it was under our horizon—it only has to be two and a half miles away in a small boat to be "hull down" —he continually looked back at the mark we had rounded and by keeping this steady on the land steered such a straight and steady course that we gained four places and never had to alter the trim of our spinnaker or mainsail.

On the reach across the Solent from the South Bramble to the East Gurnard Buoy we gained two more places and rounded third. It was now a short and simple spinnaker run to the finish with a fair tide, so we finished third, well content.

Wednesday came in with a light northerly wind pulling off the southern shores of England: the night breeze. I knew full well that at noon by the sun—1.0 p.m. B.S.T.—when the hot air of England ascended, this would die away and the day breeze make in as the cool breeze was sucked in from the sea. In the Mediterranean this change is at 10.0 a.m. as the land, being nearer to the Equator' heats up that much earlier.

The ebb tide was away and we were started to westward, though the light northerly air had by now been replaced by a calm. This tide of one and a half knots would give us, in effect, a one-and-a-half-knot breeze dead ahead; so our little boats would sail to and fro on the tide, close-hauled, going to windward with just steerage way. As there was no wind at the start, we had to keep paddling against the tide until the five-minute gun, keeping well clear of the line on the tide side, for if we were over it we could never get back and take part in the race. So I purposely made a late start.

There were sixteen of us in Flying Fifteens and we were one of the last to cross the line. As we quietly tacked to and fro on this wind given to us by the movement of the tide to windward I sailed 45° to the tide and then came about. Then I sailed 45° to the tide the other side, picking up many places on the Flying Fifteens who did not understand that this tide was giving us a wind equal to its speed. As we neared the buoy, the first breeze began to come, and where before I had been afraid of being swept by the tide outside the Royal Yacht Squadron's Buoy in Gurnard Bay, we could now sail outside it, take the stronger tide there, and so go a little faster. We rounded the buoy about two-thirds down our fleet.

Here we were amongst the Dragons, Redwings, and the Swallows: in fact all the boats that had started long before us, for with no wind they could not sail across or against the ebb tide. We were in a heap of about fifty boats. If there had been no tide it would have been a fairly close reach for our next mark across the Solent on the north shore, N.E. Gurnard; but because there was a tide this was turned into a spinnaker run. Before setting our spinnaker I asked John to roll up the jib and put a half-hitch round it with the jibsheets, so that when we needed it he had only to pull on the jibsheets to release the sail. He rolled it up quite neatly, tucking in bits of the jib as far as he could reach in between the jib luff and the forestay so that it would stay secure.

Now we were sailing with the mainsail only and while John secured the jib I was looking round for a hole in the fleet of fifty boats, through which to escape, for, with only the mainsail set, I could carry out any manœuvre on any point of sailing single-handed. When the jib was half-rolled-up I discovered a hole in the boats and changed course 180°, nipped out through it, and found a clear wind. We now set our spinnaker and started reaching across the Solent—not for our mark but to windward of it so that we could keep our clear wind, not only of the fifty boats we were in amongst now but of those ahead that we would catch up.

Away we slid across for the north shore and the easier tide over there. Striking the coast at about half a mile down-tide of our buoy we went in close, running up in the slack water round Standsoar Point as only here could we make headway against the sluicing tide. It was now 1 o'clock—noon by the sun—and about time for the day breeze to take a firm hold. At what I judged to be the right moment, I started to sail out into the stronger tide to meet this stronger south-wester and to shorten the miles up between us and the Ryde Middle Buoy: for while undoubtedly the fastest way to this buoy with no wind was on a great circle course all up the New Forest shore, if there was wind enough to push you over the tide, the more direct course would pay. So we steered for Thorn Knoll, still over the bank and out of the main ebb from Southampton Water; soon we were over the Bramble Bank, and as the tide always runs fastest in the deepest water, we continued to sail over it, not quite towards our mark.

By now the breeze had taken a firm hold, and a green Flying Fifteen that had sailed a direct course was now able to sail against the full ebb quite fast. He was almost as fast as we were in the slacker water, because he was in the stronger wind to the south and we watched him a mile and a half to windward of us. As we watched we realised that he would round the Ryde Middle Buoy ahead of us; and though running over the tide we kept our spinnaker up till we were at the buoy itself, he rounded well ahead—fifty yards.

When racing, the leader should always keep between the other boats and the next mark, with special attention to the second and third boats. After we had escaped through the hole in the fifty boats, we were the leader of the Flying Fifteens, but you cannot cover a fleet of sixteen boats when they are spread over some two miles of the course. This boat, sailing a course two miles apart from ours, well deserved her victory, for once round Ryde Middle Buoy, in a slashing south-wester and a fair tide under her, she held us in second place to the finish, as she covered every move we made, keeping between us, the wind, and the finishing-line, right to the end; so we for our part were quite content to be second.

This day the tide was more important than the wind; until 1 o'clock when the wind had freshened to the usual day breeze brought about by the land—heated by the sun—burning up the air, which had to be replaced by air drawn in from off the sea.

Thursday came in with a light northerly, but the sky was overcast which meant that, as the land would not be heated up until late afternoon, the sea breeze would not make until this time. Our triangular course was from the Island Sailing Club line, round the West Ryde, against the tide and then, with a fair tide round the South Bramble and the Gurnard Ledge Buoy and home against the tide to Cowes and the finishing-line.

With a light northerly air and a lot of moored yachts it was as usual difficult to know which part of the line to start from. If you were to windward you had your wind clear of the other boats but you had a stronger tide against you. No one at the start knew which was best until we reached Old Castle Point where the one boat that had started well inshore, well to leeward of everybody else, broke through and quietly glided ahead, and had a long lead by the time we were at Old Castle Point. Here all the racers in this class were bunched more closely together than they had been over the starting-line, so the race virtually started again for all, with the exception of the leading boat.

We were all still well inshore quietly stemming the tide when I decided to have a dart at the buoy and take the northern edge of the fleet with a clear wind. This at once started everybody going out to the buoy; and with our spinnakers pulling merrily we drove on out and were fortunate enough to be sixth round the Ryde West Middle. We had to keep our spinnaker up once again until we were actually at the buoy, in order to stem the tide. But this made little difference as once round I shot her up into the wind although the spinnaker was only half down and the tide swiftly took us to windward and we went through into fourth place. In the process we passed two boats which had rounded ahead of us, but which made the mistake of bearing away to get their spinnakers in, and in doing this sailing away from and not towards the next mark.

After we had straightened out our sails I stood over on the starboard tack towards the Island shore, but soon discovered that the boats to the north of us were gaining, as the wind was shifting more northerly. So we decided to stand to the north of the fleet to take advantage of this.

We were sailing along to the north of all the boats behind, and then, just to play safe, tacked to starboard once more, to cover them all with the exception of 126, the *Black Flame*. You cannot cover every boat in a race so I decided to let her go and take advantage of this northerly shift. We gained on the rest of the fleet under our lee but *Black Flame* passed out ahead of us when we next met and so we were fourth once again, rounding the South Bramble Buoy.

Now we had to cross half the width of the Solent with a sluicing ebb. I bore away, and slid through the lee of this black boat which held too high on the wind: and so we went along driving down on the west-going tide. As we approached Gurnard Ledge the wind fell right away to a flat calm and then came an anxious time, with a 2-m.p.h. westerly air caused by our driving to the west on this 2-knot tide. We tacked to port and starboard just altering the

This beautiful vessel, the Earl of Crawford's square-rigged *Valhalla*, travelled far and wide across the Seven Seas; by steam as well as by sail (the funnel is easily visible). The whaleboat hung in her davits was later presented to the Cowes Sea Scouts, and sometimes it took us right across the Channel to la belle France.

The 30 square-metre *Avocet* smoking along in a strong breeze. The genoa jib comes back to the end of the main boom, so that a lot of sail is set on a short mast. With their little cabins these are wonderful racing cruisers.

This picture of the Big Five—*White Heather*, the Royal Yacht *Britannia*, the schooner *Westward*, *Shamrock* and *Lulworth*—shows how fast they sailed on a wind in light airs.

In this little cruiser, *Wanderer III*, Eric Hiscock and his wife Susan have been right round the world, and here they are off once more. The boat is sturdy and strong, and has the generous displacement required for carrying food and water and everything else you need to sail the Seven Seas (see p. 147).

Flying Fox, which I designed for Fred Brownley of Ireland. Her displacement is half that of a normal cruiser and she has the ability to plane, but since she is a cruiser this only happens occasionally and is rather terrifying, though quite comfortable. Her home port now is Genoa, where there are often good winds for her to revel in.

The Hon. Max Aitken's *Drumbeat* with her spinnaker set to make the most of the wind; on this point of sailing she has proved invincible. She has already taken part in Fastnet and Bermuda races and has sailed the Atlantic. In 1960 she took part in the Bermuda race once more, but was dismasted in the race from Bermuda across the Western Ocean to Sweden.

Frank Beken, our greatest marine photographer, once pointed out to the late Chris Ratsey how much wind was being lost under his spinnaker when it was flying high. Chris immediately made what he called a "sneaker"—a light balloon staysail set under the spinnaker. Here it is being used on *Columbia*, the successful defender of the America's Cup in 1958.

Catamarans have been sailing in the South Pacific for thousands of years, and have lately become popular in northern waters too. Here is *Golden Miller*, steered by her designer, Mike Henderson. She has ballasted fin keels and a float at the top of her mast, to prevent a complete capsize.

buoy on the land to left and right as we tacked, knowing full well
that we were going almost directly at it on the tide because of this.
Finally we stood over on the starboard tack, rounded the Gurnard
Ledge Buoy and started to reach southward for the slack water
inshore.

We were going in merrily with two Flying Fifteens under our
lee and the three of us could have slid away from the fleet in this
freak of wind, but then these two came to windward and started to
attack me so we luffed them and ourselves out of this narrow
streak of wind into the calm, destroying ourselves and them and
finally dropping behind the boats, which until then had been
astern of us.

We crept on inshore and dropped our anchor and then dived
overboard and had a swim without a stitch on, leaving our Flying
Fifteen riding to her anchor with no one on board. Some years ago
I had asked the R.Y.A. to reinstate the old rule to say that a person could join or leave a ship during a race; and had it not been
for this we could have been disqualified for leaving our vessel.
After several swims we decided to dry out and then thought we
had better start trying to sail again so we pulled the kedge up; just
fanning ourselves along with the flapping of our mainsail.

As we looked way down to westward we could see boats bring-
ing up the day's westerly breeze five miles away. So we made our
spinnaker all ready and at the right moment, set it and came right
up to the two Flying Fifteens ahead of us. One of these tried to
sail through the lee of four boats and was left behind. Then we
started luffing out into the tide, and the leading Flying Fifteen
luffed out with us; which was exactly what the doctor ordered, as
at this moment we gybed, shaping our course for the Squadron, as
we were now at *Egypt* Point and this meant that this Flying Fifteen
was out into a stronger adverse tide—while he thought he was
luffing out on our weather because we were at this point altering
course 20°, he was actually sailing out under our lee. So we sailed
through into first place.

Now we came on and on up past the Green closing up with some
sixty boats ahead of us trying to find a gap through them, and there
it was, between two Dragons. A little Cherub darted in there but
stayed only for a minute before departing and we sailed through,

I

for the Dragons, I knew, would steer a fairly steady course. So we stormed up to the finishing-line, all of us bustling along briskly as the tide had now eased and the westerly was sparkling. It was the race officers nightmare—all classes finishing together. We came to the finishing-line, weather, inside, and leading Flying Fifteen.

So ended a wonderfully enjoyable race. After we had finished the westerly wind once more swung north-west and finally north, as the haze never allowed the land to heat up enough to bring in the normal strong south-wester.

The Friday of Cowes Week is always the Cowes Town Regatta day, and the sailing races start at 10.0 a.m. across a line only 200 yards westward of the Royal Yacht Squadron line so that all Town Regatta classes are clear of the starting-line and scattered all over the Solent before the Royal Squadron start their regatta.

The day came in with a light easterly breeze. The Flying Fifteen start was at 10.50 and although the first of the ebb tide had started close under the shore the flood tide was still flowing strongly outside. So as our start was to the east with a fair flood tide there was no doubt that the outer end was the place from which to start, as on the inner end we had the west-going eddy. Then the thing to do was to stand out to sea until we could make Old Castle Point, the first buoy, in one tack; and this we planned to do. Unfortunately, I missed a minute in our five-minute manœuvring time and was a minute late arriving on the line at its outer mark. So we went away ninth boat over the line and though we stood right out in the tide, farther to the north than anyone else, we were still ninth when we rounded Old Castle Point.

Now it was a spinnaker run to the South Bramble Buoy with the spinnaker to starboard against the flood tide, and we kept well to leeward of the fleet and, quietly, with a clear wind, ploughed through them thanks to the wonderful handling of the spinnaker on the part of John, my crew. We generally only sail together three to five times a year and this was our fifth race together so we had now settled down with each other. It must be remembered that while helmsmen are ten a penny good crews are pearls beyond price. All a helmsman has to do is sit and steer, but a good crew has to have a vast knowledge of a great many things.

And seldom are the conditions of sail-handling the same for a crew. The wind and tide are different; we take in the spinnaker and gybe or we take it in and tack, and the sail-handling and trimming are most important and difficult throughout. On this occasion I was blessed with a good crew, which enabled me to execute any manœuvre in the twinkling of an eye.

Looking at the fleet I could see that most of them had their spinnakers sheeted too tight. You must always have your spinnaker flying so that its luff is on edge and often drops in a little, perhaps through the helmsman altering course slightly. So with our spinnaker on edge and with a clear wind down to leeward, we went from ninth into first place on this run. We increased this lead on the next run against the tide from the South Bramble Buoy to the East Gurnard, and, because it was a flood tide again, we kept the spinnaker up until we were right past the buoy.

As I shot the boat into and on the wind, the spinnaker, of course, flew aft. The crew, not expecting this and realising that we were already round the buoy, gathered in the spinnaker now flying a long way to leeward, but this did not matter as we had a strong flood pushing us to windward, and directly our spinnaker was down, we tacked out into the even stronger tide and then made another tack to port across the line—an easy winner.

With our win on this, the fifth and final day of the Flying Fifteen Cowes Week Championship, our score was three firsts, a second and a third. *Coweslip* was easily top boat, and John and I were delighted. It had been a light-weather week, and here were we, two fairly heavy chaps weighing 14 stone each in our clothes— and the boat *Coweslip*, in which we were racing for the Duke of Edinburgh, ten years old and heavier than many of her newer sisters. This showed that although weight is not a good thing, it does no harm in light airs; for though a heavy boat takes longer to get going, once she is on the move she keeps her momentum longer, and will often glide through a calm patch which will trap the lighter boat that loses its way quickly. The great moment for the light boat is when there is just enough wind to make her plane and not enough wind to lift the heavier one out of the water.

As I have said, I was fortunate in my crew, and after the first two races we had settled down to each other and hardly needed to speak about sailing once we had started racing. Instead, we could yarn enjoyably about all sorts of things—houses, horses, life, and so on. Of the four units that make for efficiency in racing —the hull, the mast and rig, the helmsman, and the crew—I would put, first and foremost, the crew; in spite of the fact that when a crew makes mistakes in sail-handling it is a matter of seconds, whereas when the helmsman makes a mistake it is often a matter of minutes.

The simplest and most enjoyable form of racing is match racing, where only two boats are racing the course. This makes the race simple and the problems simple—you have only to beat the other, whereas in fleets of over a dozen you not only have to sail better than twelve other boats but it is impossible, when in the lead, to cover all the fleet. We never once made a good start during this Week, and were generally well down the fleet rounding the first mark; but before ever we started I had a yarn to my crew and outlined the general strategy of the race and this we followed, as closely as we could, and only altered it at different points on the spur of the moment when other boats and conditions demanded new tactics. This meant that we never had to make a hasty decision, particularly when off the wind, and therefore it is wise to look over the course, appreciating every single situation well in advance and making a plan. Even a bad plan, well carried-out, often succeeds, whereas if you have no plan you can have no hope of success. Nothing in this world is perfect; everything can be improved; and in every race different helmsmen had made better starts than I had. But as we all make mistakes it necessarily follows that the man who makes the least number of them must win the race. Sailing a race can be likened to living our lives; we must learn to strive and not to yield; for failure is not in falling down, but in not getting up and continuing.

I have said earlier that the way to win races is to sail your own boat as clear of the rest of the fleet as possible; in this way you avoid collisions and arguments, make yourself into a little isolated kingdom of your own with your own rules, and have only your own kingdom to consider. Only then can you get the utmost out of your boat. I have always struggled to go off on my own even if it is to a place where there is less wind and a stronger, adverse tide, for the very fact that you are alone enables you to concentrate on your boat, her sails and gear, and your own steering. And throughout Cowes Week of 1959 we were never in close conflict with any other boat for more than a few seconds, such as at the start when it could not be avoided, and rounding marks. The result of that week's racing shows how sensible it is to sail your own ship apart from the fleet. The old R.Y.A. Number One rule lays it down that you must strive to win your races by the magic of seamanship and steersmanship; and wise is the man who keeps this as his first and most important commandment.

It was calm weather throughout the Week; on the days when there was a clear sky at eleven o'clock we could see what we call the "little messengers", going up a long way off in the centre of England, although the early morning northerly breeze was still pulling off the land. Then we knew that as these little clouds were the top of rising currents so, within a few hours, the wind would be sucked in off the sea, and the hotter the day the brisker this breeze would become. We also knew that if it was hazy and cloudy it would form a sunshade and England would not get heated up, and therefore would not want to suck in the fresh sea breeze, so this would not make until late in the day and even then would have very little strength. So as well as looking at the water and things at eye-level we should always look at the sky above, as this has a great deal to tell those who will look, listen and understand.

Finally, sailing races are similar to examinations; when the examination is over the class can be graded by its knowledge of different subjects, and when a race is over the fleet can also be graded into its knowledge of wind, weather and boat-handling. Against this must be balanced the physical strength and weight of those taking part; for although women are the equal of men in their knowledge of the sea, winds and vessels, and can win races in the light weather that is well within their strength, they cannot hope to defeat men in heavy blowing weather, when great strength as well as knowledge is required. By racing you not only improve your sailing ability, but you have your standard of ability set out to you by your position in the fleet.

VI

Cruising

HAVING learnt to sail and, through racing, improved our standard of sailing and understanding of the ways of wind and wave, we can now go cruising.

Cruising is great fun, and I have vivid and happy memories of it; for although every so often gales, calms, tide rips or rocks cause anxious moments, the delightful hours far outweigh all the others. In our vessel we are a little kingdom separated from the rest of the world and completely cut off; no letters, no papers, no telephone. Without a care in our hearts we can choose the place where we would be and go there; we can choose our neighbours, and leave them whenever we wish. But just as we must feel hungry to enjoy a meal, so must we have an anxiety to enjoy the peace of the sea. Cruising as a sport or a way of life brings contentment and happiness. Great possessions and wealth do not necessarily bring happiness, neither do we have to have a great yacht in order to cruise; we can enjoy cruising in whatever vessel we are able to afford.

Generally speaking, when we are young, our pocket-money is small, our wants are easily filled, and we are very happy. When I was young I designed and built myself a little ten-foot rowing and sailing dinghy, and in her I went cruising in the summer and used her for sailing and rowing through the autumn, winter and spring. She carried camping gear so that I could either sleep in her with the sails over the boom, or rig a tent ashore. She was a full-bodied boat, which not only enabled her to carry my cruising gear as well as me, but also gave her steadiness and stability. Because of the fullness of her lines I named her *The Brave Alum Bey* from one of W. S. Gilbert's Bab Ballads, "O Big was the Bosom of Brave Alum Bey, and also the region that under it lay".

In her I cruised and enjoyed the waters of the Wight, and as far west as Lulworth Cove.

At another period I designed and built a little cruising canoe, 16 ft. long and 2 ft. 9 in. wide. These little boats brought me a great deal of happiness and carried me safely hundreds of miles. But the larger the boat the more gear you can carry, until finally you get the cruising vessel with full headroom. Then you have the freedom of the seas, for a small boat cannot carry water and food enough to make her independent of the land for more than a few hours. It is essential to be able to stand upright; so the smallest possible cruiser is some 24-ft. waterline, which is about the shortest waterline length that will give you 6 ft. of headroom.

A 24-ft. waterline is the minimum length for a sea-keeping cruiser for the following reasons:

(a) When sailing close-hauled the speed of a boat is the square root of her waterline length and a 24-ft. waterline boat will use a 25-ft. waterline once she starts to move. Five is the square root of twenty-five and five knots is quite slow enough to sail when cruising; in the past most cruisers have tended to starve rather than drown their owners.

(b) We cannot get 6 ft. of headroom on a well-proportioned boat with less than 24 ft. waterline.

(c) Whether in a small or large boat, people still require living space and the capacity to carry food, water, bedding and clothing. In fact the shorter and slower the boat, the more food and water required.

So *Cambria*, designed for Wales, is the minimum-sized, sensible cruiser.

Length Overall: 31' (9·500m)   *Length Waterline:* 24' (7·316m)
Beam: 10' 3" (3·084m)   *Draught:* 5' 6" (1·676m)
Displacement: 4·75 *tons* (4,826   *Sail Area:* 476 *sq. ft.* (44 *sq. m*)
    kilos)

Now although her draft is normal (5 ft 6 in.) her displacement of 5 tons is just on the light side for such a vessel. But if she were going on a long cruise and taking a lot of stores on board, she

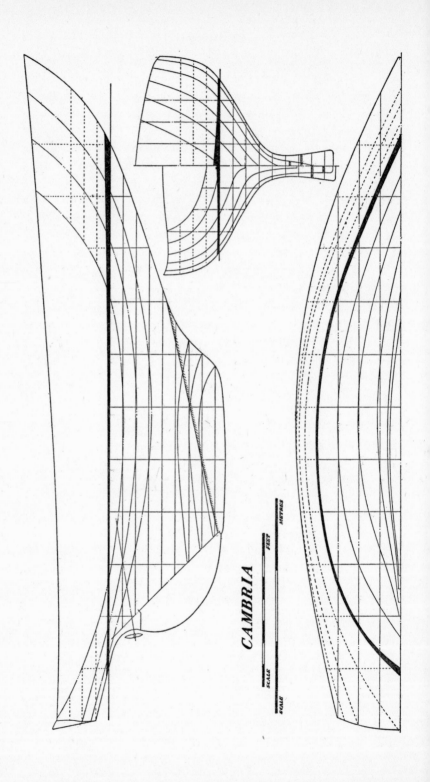

CAMBRIA

SCALE

FEET

SCALE

METRES

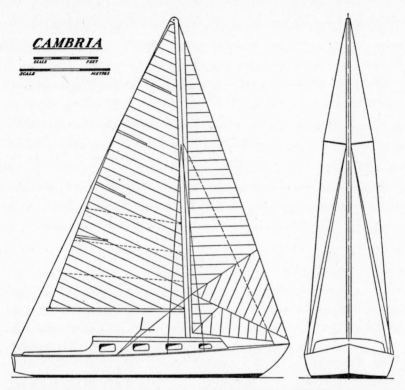

<figure>
CAMBRIA

SCALE   FEET

SCALE   METRES
</figure>

Sail Plan: The mast is supported permanently in all directions. The jib stay, back stay and main shrouds hold the masthead steady and the four lower shrouds leading directly to the deck are spread well fore and aft as well as athwartships so steady the mast at this height. The portable forestay is set up only in blowing weather. A good rig to go to sea with.

(Left) **Lines (deep keel):** These lines are fine and easily driven, the beam increasing with the length; the bilge is above the waterline, so her stability and power grow quickly as extra loading is put on her.

would soon pick up extra displacement, for her bilge is above the waterline. So she quickly increases her waterline beam and displacement as she is pushed deeper into the water and this is a good thing in a little vessel. It will be noted that her ballast keel is wider at the bottom than at the top. This has two results: it gets the weight of the ballast lower where it does more good and, as no vessel sails upright but heels to leeward, it also keeps the side of her keel more plumb than usual when heeled, giving her more grip and not reducing her draft quite so much when she is heeled. The buttocks, waterlines and sections all tell of a very easily-driven vessel and though she has a moderate sail area, she should go along quite well in light weather while at the same time her wide high bilge enables her to be driven hard in a breeze of wind.

The sail-plan shows that her mainboom is only 15 ft. long so she has an easily-handled mainsail of 225 sq. ft., practically the same size as her 240-sq. ft. genoa which, by Royal Ocean Racing Club rules, can overlap the mast half the distance the mast is from the forestay. So with her sail area almost equally divided between genoa and mainsail, handling problems are fairly simple, and with only four sails we have combinations to suit all winds, from a calm to a 50-m.p.h. gale, as can be seen from the set of six sail-pans on page 56.

Cambria can carry her mainsail and genoa—a total area of 476 sq. ft.—in winds up to 22 m.p.h. After this she should change to a jib and staysail, which not only reduces the sail area to 448 sq. ft., but also spreads the load on to two stays and two different parts of the mast. Moreover, as the headsail area is split in two this also eases the strain on the crew, and there will not be such a sag in the jib stay as the jib is only just over half the area of the genoa. At 26 m.p.h. she should take in her staysail and reduce the area to 367 sq. ft. The next change down will come when the wind rises to 33 m.p.h., when she changes from the jib to her staysail and reefs her main, reducing the area to 264 sq. ft. which also brings the centre of sail pressure down some 3 ft. For a wind of 37 m.p.h. the second reef in the mainsail reduces the area to 225 sq. ft.; finally, dowsing her staysail and hauling down the third reef in the mainsail, she has only 110 sq. ft., for a 50 m.p.h. gale with all on board wishing they were in some snug harbour and that the gale would soon abate.

The mast is well into the boat, one-third of the waterline from its fore end, where it can be easily carried. If it were too far forward the mainsail pressure would bury the bow, and if too far aft the boat would not be steerable under mainsail only. It is held firmly at all times by permanent rigging in all directions. At the masthead the forestay and the main backstay hold it steady in the fore and aft direction, while the main shrouds from the masthead over crosstrees hold it steady athwartships. Just above half height there are four lower shrouds—two at each side—and these not only hold the mast firmly athwartships but, because they are spread well fore and aft of it, also hold it steady in a fore and aft direction. The one disadvantage is that the lower shrouds, extending forward, make it more difficult in tacking to get the sheets and the headsails round. On the other hand, the mast is secure in all directions and here we see a rig permanently held in place by the eight members of its standing rigging without the need of runners that have to be continually slacked off and set up.

On all the masthead rigs I've sailed, the top has bent and moved a lot in its fore and aft direction, so this mast is without taper fore and aft, and only tapered sideways, as here the main shrouds with their crosstrees give great support athwartships. The mainsail is roller reefing, so the round mainboom is larger at its outer end; then, when three reefs are taken in, this end is 18 in. higher than with full sail as it is lifted 6 in. higher with every reef. For the seas increase with the wind and we should always keep our boom end out of the water in blowing weather.

The fo'c'sle has a built-in berth that can be used in harbour, and should only be used at sea in fine weather, as here you are at the outer end of a see-saw where the motion is most violent and there is all the swish of the waves to keep you awake. To port there is a little washroom; to starboard a large full-length wardrobe. Immediately abaft is the mast and the main cabin, with a folding table and a bunk at either side for sleeping or sitting, and books above the backrests. Dividing this from the cockpit is the galley to port, and the chartroom to starboard—the best arrangement

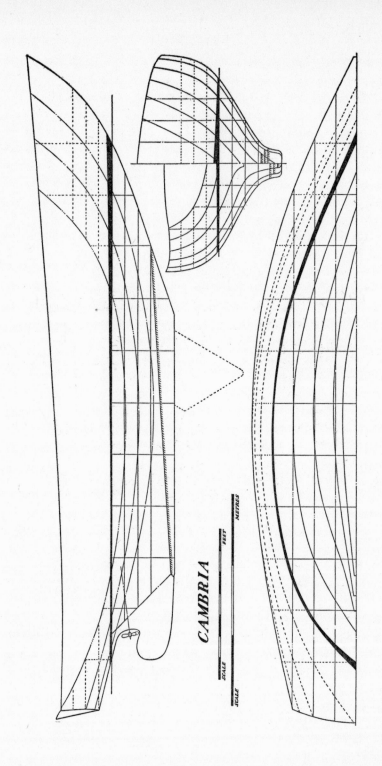

CAMBRIA

SCALE

FEET

SCALE

METRES

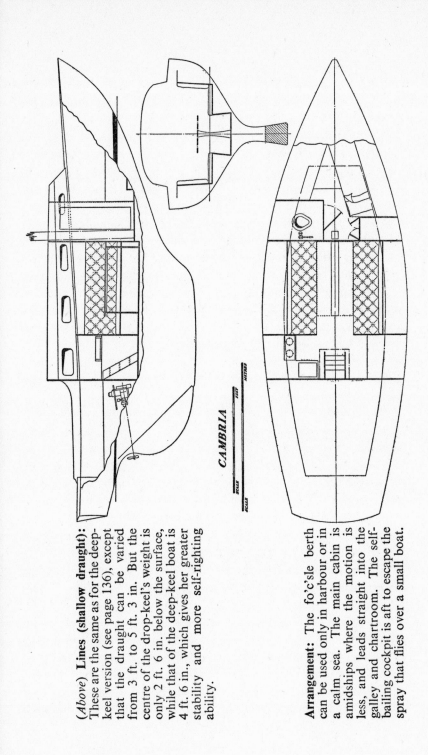

CAMBRIA

SCALE

FEET
METRES

(*Above*) **Lines (shallow draught):** These are the same as for the deep-keel version (see page 136), except that the draught can be varied from 3 ft. to 5 ft. 3 in. But the centre of the drop-keel's weight is only 2 ft. 6 in. below the surface, while that of the deep-keel boat is 4 ft. 6 in., which gives her greater stability and more self-righting ability.

Arrangement: The fo'c'sle berth can be used only in harbour or in a calm sea. The main cabin is amidships where the motion is less, and leads straight into the galley and chartroom. The self-bailing cockpit is aft to escape the spray that flies over a small boat.

for small boats, as here they are in the centre of the see-saw and the motion is least. Here, cooking can be carried on in most weathers and meals either served straight on to the dining-table or out into the cockpit, depending on whether you are eating in the open or below. The chart-table, being immediately inside the cockpit, enables a man sailing single-handed to have his charts within reach. The cockpit is self-bailing and the drains aft, through the transom. So even if the drainpipes should be broken the vessel would not sink, as you can drive the plug in the transom and stop any water coming through. The coachroof not only gives full headroom, but also affords shelter for those in the cockpit. Some people favour a cockpit amidships and although this has advantages in that it divides the accommodation in two, there is a great deal of spray flying over the centre of a vessel and you get much wetter in a midship cockpit than in one that is aft. This accommodation plan follows the general practice in vessels of this size and has proved the best through the years.

Not everyone wishes to use or can use to advantage a deep-keeled vessel, so I have designed another version of the same boat which draws only 3 ft. of water (see page 140).

This boat has many advantages. It can lie on the mud, sand or shore without heeling over to any extent; and with its drop-keel hoisted, it can go into rivers, harbours, and creeks that a deep-keeled boat could not attempt. Off the wind with the drop-keel up its wetted surface is cut down to a minimum, which makes for more speed. But you cannot have these advantages without losing something. Where the centre of the ballast keel in a deep-keel draft is low down, the centreboard boat's ballast keel is only just under water; so the centreboard boat cannot stand up to the hard driving to windward in a seaway or to the same wind pressure as a deep-keeled boat, a point which should always be borne in mind when sailing centreboard craft.

The hull lines, accommodation, masting, rigging and sail-plans, are the same for both boats, the only difference between them being in their draft of water and ultimate stability. Their general speed and performance will be much the same for, whereas the keel-boat will drive faster to windward, the centreboard version will chase away before the wind at a higher speed. The centreboard boat has a

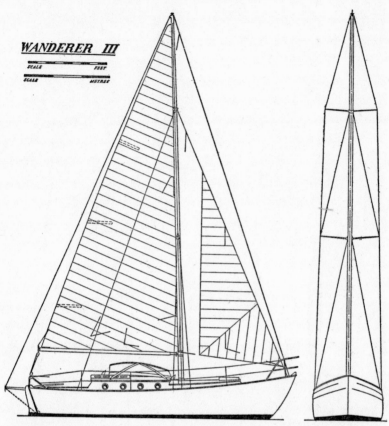

WANDERER III

Sail Plan: The masthead rig is supported fore and aft by the jib and forestays, a permanent topmast backstay to a bumkin aft and a pair of runners; and sideways by two pairs of shrouds over two pairs of cross-trees and four lower shrouds. There are four different size headsails with the mainsail and trysail, as well as running sails, so she is equipped for all types of weather and all points of sailing.

(*Left*) **Lines:** A full-bodied vessel with her bilge well below the waterline and able to carry a great deal of stores; at the same time her long keel makes her easy to steer and comfortable to sail in.

K

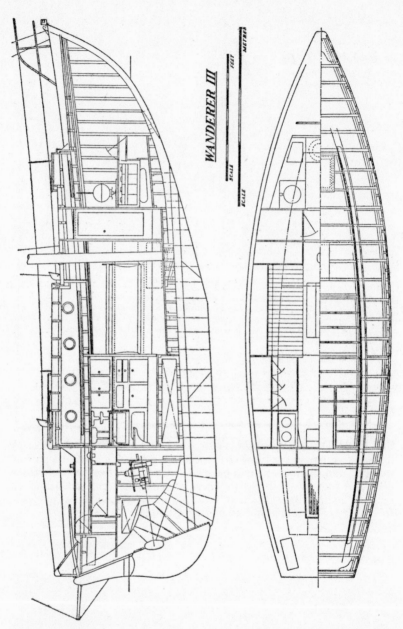

Arrangement: The small cockpit is self-bailing and the galley is well aft in the quietest part of the vessel. The ballast keel is amidships so that she lifts her ends to the seas.

Wanderer III

Length Overall: 30′ 3″ (9·220m)   *Length Waterline:* 26′ 6″ (8·077m)
Beam: 8′ 5″ (2·565m)   *Draught:* 5′ (1·525m)
Displacement: 7 tons (7,112 *kilos*)   *Sail Area:* 600 sq. ft. (55·75 sq. m)

Eric C. Hiscock and his wife have cruised round the world in this wonderful vessel taking three years over the voyage. The boat cost £3,000 to build in 1951 and Eric Hiscock, her owner and skipper, reckons it costs £500 a year to run her, including food, repairs, upkeep, in fact everything. Which proves once more the old maxim that it is cheap to go to sea as long as you stay there.

On such a voyage, and over three years, every kind of weather is experienced, from heavy gales with great seas to calms: so we see it is not the size, so much as the design, that makes for seaworthiness. I am fortunate enough to be able to reproduce in this book the lines of this wonderful little vessel through the kindness of her designer, Laurent Giles, M.R.I.N.A., R.D.I. Now, after two years at his home in the Isle of Wight, Eric and his wife have once more put to sea for another long voyage in the same ship, which shows their contentment with her, their faith and trust remaining unchanged after two years of contemplation. A quiet study of her plans will repay anyone wishing to cruise, for here is a little vessel that has sailed the Seven Seas and gone through the fire seven times.

We see in the plans of *Wanderer III* ideas for a world-girdling vessel, for she was designed for that purpose. The lines, though clean, fair and sweet to the eye, are those of a full-bodied boat. She has in her main fresh-water-tank 30 gallons of water, and in two others 15 gallons each, with 10-gallon jerrycans in the forepeak to give a total of 70 gallons of water. There is food and clothing for two people for such a voyage, navigational gear, radio sets, a little library and all the things needed for a three-year stay away from home, with spells of up to one month at sea.

The accommodation shows a W.C. in the fore end, twin berths on either side of the main saloon, and abaft this the galley to port and the chart-table to starboard, a self-bailing cockpit aft and under this a 4-h.p. Stuart Turner engine.

As well as all this she carries two 35-lb. anchors, 45 fathoms of chain and two 30-fathom 2-in. warps.

Eric Hiscock chose a masthead cutter rig, a rig that sets the maximum area of sail on the shortest possible mast, a sensible one for a seagoing vessel. Also, the permanent backstay aft ensures that the mast will stand steady in all weathers.

Her mast is well into her, making her an easy boat in a head sea and keeping the mainsail small; so that all early reefing is done by changing the headsails down to a smaller size. The sail-plan shows that she has a genoa jib of the maximum size allowed by the Royal Ocean Yacht Club rules, and three staysails decreasing in size. So with four different-sized headsails, she can pick the right one for most weathers; then, after reducing sail by this method, she can start reefing her mainsail with its roller reefing gear. Finally, in a heavy gale, this can be taken in and her storm trysail set. The mast is $7\frac{1}{4}$ in. by $5\frac{5}{8}$ in., tapering to $3\frac{3}{4}$ in. by $3\frac{3}{4}$ in. at the top. The wall thickness of this hollow spar is $1\frac{1}{2}$ in. for the lower portion, tapering away to $1\frac{1}{8}$ in. at the top, and this spar is supported by two sets of crosstrees, one at the staysail halyard heights and the other approximately halfway between this and the deck. Her lower and cap shrouds are an inch in circumference.

So here we have a perfect little ocean cruiser that has proved her worth, and Eric Hiscock and his wife, Susan, by their quiet, enduring courage have also proved beyond all doubt that, not only is such a little ship a wonderful sea-boat, but also a home comfortable enough to live in for three or more years. And in so doing they have helped and encouraged sailing people the world over.

The Rig to Go to Sea

Once we start cruising we can go to the uttermost ends of the earth, as our ship—provided she has enough food and water and is quite sound and staunchly rigged—can plough her lonely furrow from England to Australia and back, or to any other land on earth. And as every land's longest distance is in its coastline we have a great choice of harbours on arrival.

It is well to remember, though, that the furrow which our little vessel ploughs is in the sea and is immediately filled in, so that afterwards there is no mark left there to say that she has passed. The seas and their winds have remained unchanged from the beginning of time; and although thousands upon thousands of vessels have cut through them there is no remembrance of them on the face of these great waters. They are often wild wastes with mighty winds blowing over them, and there is no place upon them to hide from this enormous and relentless power; no rock or cliff to crouch behind. Our vessels and we, ourselves, must stand up to whatever winds the Lord sends us. Therefore, we must choose not only a stout vessel, but also a sensible and seaworthy rig.

When I was young and lusty I could handle, in all weathers, 500 sq. ft. of sail, and some forty years ago I laid down the law that, if possible, no cruising vessel should have her largest sail with more than 500 sq. ft. in it. Then, even if there was only one man, active and able, aboard, this sail could be handled. Of course the smaller the sail the more easy it is to handle, and now that so many of the gentle sex sail—who cannot handle one of more than 250 sq. ft. in a gale—I have drawn out six rigs to illustrate the sizes of ships they can manage single-handed. And as illness might overtake all aboard except one woman, the largest sail in every case is close on 250 sq. ft. (see p. 151).

The cutter is the most efficient and the staysail schooner the most seaworthy and the strongest of these rigs. I value the cutter rig at 100%, the yawl rig at 95%, and both the schooner and the ketch at 85%. So the only reason for going to a rig other than the cutter is for the ease of handling sails in heavy weather and the security of the rig. There is no doubt that the staysail schooner rig, having two masts supporting each other and spreading the loads of the vessel over two spars instead of over one and having no runners to let go or set up, is the strongest and the easiest to handle and therefore makes for the greatest security at sea.

So to begin with we have the cutter rig, with its great efficiency, but with all the loads and strains coming on to one mast and in one part of the vessel. Then we have the yawl rig in which some of the strain has been transferred to the mizzen, well aft. Next we come to the ketch rig, with its larger mizzen spreading the loads still more but even so, with neither mast supporting or strengthening the other, for it is impossible to do so with this rig with any degree of efficiency and safety. Now we come to the gaff schooner rig and here the masts do support each other, but not permanently, as you must let the runners go on the mainmast, so you are still not altogether safe and secure. Then we come to my favourite rig, the staysail schooner. Here you have both masts tied securely together, with the stays running from the stemhead over both mastheads and down to the stern, securing everything fore and aft without any danger of losing either stick and with the loads spread fairly evenly over both spars. Finally, we have the wishbone ketch; a rig that is quite efficient and yet has never really taken on, although it has won races across the Atlantic and allows you to have a larger vessel than any of the other rigs for the same effort and strength on the part of the crews.

Were I choosing a vessel, I should have for first choice, cutter rig, then for real sea-going work the staysail schooner rig, and a yawl rig as the third favourite. This set of six sail-plans shows how the size of vessel can be increased by using different rigs.

The other limiting factor for size is the anchor, for the two things that call for the greatest strength on any vessel are:

(*a*) The reefing, stowing and handling of her largest sail.

(*b*) The heaving up and safe stowage of her anchor and chain.

Time and time again it is not the anchor that needs heaving up but the anchor chain, for when we anchor in deep water there is a terrific weight in the length of chain hanging up and down from the stemhead and from our vessel herself sitting back on the chain through the weight of wind and tide. The sea is never still, so whenever we have an anchor chain up and down that is heavy, or we have to break it out of the ground, we should make our work easier by heaving away on our capstan or winch as the vessel is descending into the hollow of the waves, and stopping as she is ascending. Finally, when the chain is hove short, the vessel—her buoyancy lifting to the sea—will break the anchor out of the ground for us and then, of course, we must wind up the rest as fast as we can.

Engines

Often when we are in harbour, and sometimes at sea as well, our vessel requires propelling by means other than sail. In my 20-tonner *Fresh Breeze* I had a deep, oval steering crutch with the top enclosed so that the oar could not jump out, and with this I would often scull her in harbour, the sweep making a figure of

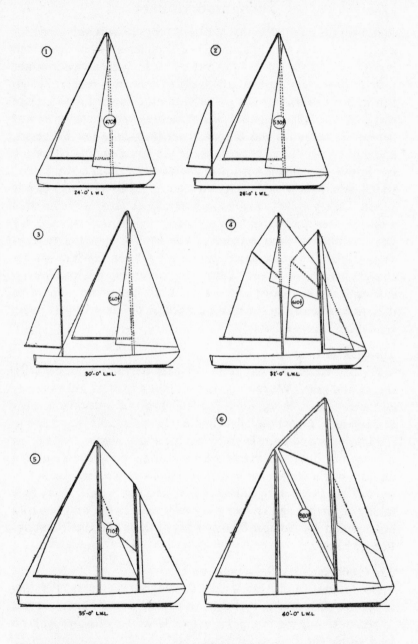

① 24'-0" L.W.L.
② 26'-0" L.W.L.
③ 30'-0" L.W.L.
④ 32'-0" L.W.L.
⑤ 35'-0" L.W.L.
⑥ 40'-0" L.W.L.

Six Sea-going Rigs: Cutter, yawl, ketch, gaff schooner, staysail schooner and wishbone ketch. The largest sail in every case is 250 sq. ft., while the total sail area varies from 470 to 980 sq. ft.

eight over the stern. But this means of propulsion is only good for a very short distance. When the late Templeman Mew, an Island brewer, owned the lovely old yawl *Coral*, he had the wisdom not only to have very narrow gangways so that only men could go below, but to dispense altogether with an engine. Instead, there was a reliable launch in his davits or on deck and whenever he was becalmed the launch was dropped over the side to tow his vessel, and directly the breeze came up again the launch would be hoisted in. In this way engine smell was avoided and room down below, which otherwise would have been taken up by the engine, was saved. On my old 20-ton schooner, the *Black Rose*, we often used a dinghy over the side with an outboard engine: with this one day we were able to sheer across the tide from Lymington to Yarmouth—steering at an angle so that the tide on the bow set her straight across the Solent. But towing or lashing a launch alongside can only be carried out in a calm sea, and as we quite often need an engine in a breeze of wind when we fit one we must choose something that is reliable.

Thoughts on Gear

For day sailing and day racing we need only our boat, her sails, sheets, and gear. We can manage without any other aid as nearly all the marks are in sight and the sailing instructions take us clear of dangers. Compasses, tidal charts, tide tables, and charts add to our efficiency and knowledge by the facts they impart, but we can manage without them. Once we go cruising, however, we need a number of these aids for within a few hours we shall be out of sight of our home port, sailing strange and new waters, every mile taking us farther and farther away over seas, rivers, and estuaries unknown to us. So now follows a list of these aids, their description and uses.

The Compass

Our foremost and greatest aid is the magnetic compass. Pointing to the magnetic North, it enables us to steer a true course out and to return to our starting point over wild wastes of water with no land visible for days and weeks on end.

The first rule for happiness and contentment on a vessel is that, whatever else you do, you must never doubt your compass. The only marriages that are completely happy are those where the husband and wife never have doubts of each other's steadfastness; this is equally true of a ship, so never doubt the steadiness and directness of your compass. All compasses are true, and will point to the magnetic North, but if you bring steel or any other magnetic metal into close contact with one, say within six feet or less, you will give it what is called deviation; which means that it is caused to deviate from the magnetic North. Sailing vessels built of wood, with copper and bronze fastenings, a lead keel, and without engines, can have no deviation as there is nothing to cause it. But most vessels today have an engine as an auxilary so, before setting off on a cruise, you should have a compass-adjuster on your vessel. He will put in compensating magnets to reduce the deviation to a minimum and then write you out a compass-card which will tell you the deviation on all points. As this varies with the different points or degrees on which you steer, it will be a very complete list and must be consulted on every change of course.

Many years ago I went to Dunkirk to bring back an 11-knot, power-driven vessel and there was no time or money to spare on getting a compass-adjuster aboard. So, as she lay in the basin, I worked her round the 360° of the compass and made my own deviation card from this, using the spire of a church and other conspicuous objects. A compass-adjuster would have been continually taking sights at the sun but I was just an ordinary mortal and reckoned that as the church steeple had stood firm for hundreds of years it would be good enough. This compass was 90° out of true, so I wrote out a deviation card: "To go West, steer North, magnetic." For I had the feeling that I might get sloshed on my one and only evening in Dunkirk and, knowing that we should leave at midnight on the tide, I had to get all this written out simply.

We left in thick weather; and after picking up the No. 4 buoy off Calais, came through the Varne Shoal without seeing its lightship; then picked up one of the buoys of the Royal Sovereign shoal without seeing that lightship either. Nor did we see the Owers or the Nab. Finally, as we approached the east end of the Isle of Wight I lowered an anchor until it was some ten feet under our bow, and steamed quietly in, knowing that the anchor would pick up Bembridge Ledge before we did. In fact, we sighted Bembridge Ledge Buoy, so all was well, and the rest was fairly easy. So this vessel, strange to me, was brought from Dunkirk into Cowes through a thick fog, and by a compass as much as 90° out, with no worry at all. Which shows how simple a compass is and how true, and how important it is not to doubt it.

The ancient mariners did not have a compass—they were mostly coasting people. The English Channel is about 100 miles wide at its western end, from Brittany to Cornwall: 50 miles wide from Cherbourg to the Isle of Wight; and only 20 miles wide from Calais to Dover. The Phoenicians used to come to Britain for the tin mined in Cornwall, and because they had no compass they did not like the hundred miles across Channel direct from Finisterre to Land's End. They would, however, do the 50 miles from Cherbourg to the Isle of Wight. I used to own Puckaster Cove which was thought to be their landing place. The Cornish tin came for the main part on pack-horses from Cornwall and across to the Isle of Wight, where it was put on board the Phoenician vessels. It must be remembered that when Julius Caesar came, he crossed the 20 miles from Calais to Dover.

The points of the early compasses of Europe were named after the winds of the Mediterranean; later they were changed to North, South, East and West, with intermediate points as well. Today the compass is marked in degrees; zero at North and round to right: East is 90°; South 180°; and West 270°. For steering at night, and for compass courses, I still prefer to use the points that are marked inside the degree ring, as this conjures up a picture of a compass direction so that you can easily see to steer north-east, or south-south-west or north-west by north. We only have to remember that the sun is south at midday, approximately east at six in the morning, west at six in the evenings, south-east at nine in the morning and south-west at three in the afternoon, and we have a fair view of the compass direction from the sun itself. In the long summer days the sun hardly goes below the horizon and even at midnight the glow of it can still be seen coming from under the sky-line to the north so that you can get a good idea of your compass direction from it.

If we were old-fashioned we would say, "Steer Tramontana,"

and if we were up-to-date we would say, "Steer on zero"; I prefer to be halfway and say, "Steer north." A rose to illustrate the compass which has the degrees on the outer ring, then the various points inside and, out beyond the degrees, the old compass points named after the winds will give its comprehensive history all in one diagram.

When steering by compass never keep your eye glued completely to it, for if your vessel is in a jerky seaway, the compass card, although it is damped down in its liquid, will swing a little on either side of true. For the most part you should watch your ship's head or mast, sight it against a cloud or light in the sky or a mark in the distance, and steer on that, checking continuously with the compass: only thus can you keep a steady course. Therefore your compass should be placed in a direct line from you, forward. If, as in most cruising vessels, you are steering with a wheel, this is fairly easy, as the compass can be arranged in front of it, where the binnacle will take up little or no room and will protect the wheel and itself and the helmsman, each one of these three helping to defend the others and all being one unit. With tiller steering, you generally sit to windward in a breeze of wind and to leeward in light weather, or one side or the other to get into the sun or the shade. So, when steering from the side you should be able to ship your compass so that it is directly ahead and you are not looking sideways at it, which makes steering difficult.

As well as guiding us with our steering and taking us where we would go, the compass can also be used to take a bearing on the sun, moon, a star, a point of land, or any other object. And by taking cross-bearings with it we can plot our position fairly accurately on a chart. For this purpose, small hand-bearing compasses are made and cost very little money. They are liquid, so quite steady and true, and have a prism to enlarge the point towards which you look. Also, in the handle, there is a little electric battery, so that by pressing a button you can illuminate them at night. It is always useful to have one of these on a boat as any time you want your faith restored in your steering compass you can take the hand-bearing one to a remote part of the vessel free from any steel or magnetism and call back the bow bearing to the man steering as a check on the steering compass.

Many men who go to sea today think it is wonderful to put great knives and huge marlinspikes in their belts. Although this is handy and makes them look tough seamen, they should never be allowed to steer, as in doing so they will bring these objects to within two feet of the compass where they can easily cause it to deviate from the true course for many miles, which could bring disaster. Although I dislike stainless steel, as it will not cut, there is non-magnetic stainless steel, and this could very well be used for marlinspikes and also for the big knives these chaps like to carry. Your compass must always be your unerring guide, and wise is the seaman who, taking care that his compass is true and never interfered with by a magnetic object, is therefore able to put his whole trust and faith in it.

Lead and Line

With a lead and line we can get the exact depth of the water. We choose lead, the densest common metal, so that it sinks quickly, and we have the thinnest line it is possible to use and handle, to reduce friction as it goes down and to stop it shrinking when wet or lengthening when drying out.

To heave the lead—if you are in a large ship and she has a fair amount of way on—you swing the lead round and round in the chains in a vertical direction and then, when it is flying out to its fullest extent forward, let go and it plunges forward, down into the sea. As the leadsman passes over it he lifts it up and down an inch or two just tapping the bottom; looks at the mark that is on the water-level and calls out the depth it shows. In smaller boats the procedure is the same but it is not necessary to whirl the lead round; you can just swing it to and fro but again, let it go when it is at its fullest extent and going forward. This is a very difficult operation and calls for a nice degree of hand and eye work, and while most of us who are right-handed can lead quite well from the starboard side, we all find it very difficult from the port side. Added to which we are generally leading while sailing close-hauled on a lee shore, when the sails, rigging, and all the boat are listing over at an angle of 45°. This makes it difficult not only to balance but also to handle the lead, for if we swing it round in the circle, or only in the lower half of a circle, the lead will be plumb and upright throughout, whereas the vessel and all her gear are at an angle. It is a wet, slippery and difficult job and very few yachtsmen ever bother to learn the art.

The expression "Swinging the Lead", meaning to shirk duty, comes from this because often, in olden times in the darkness of night, the leadsmen would call the depth without letting the lead go out of his hand. To heave the lead is to throw it into the sea as far as possible ahead of the ship when it is underway; but, if you have to take a sounding in deep water and want to be accurate, you must first get all the way off your ship and then lower your lead down to the bottom. The 28-lb. deep-sea lead line is used in depths up to 200 fathoms, and is marked by a large knot at every 10 fathoms and a small one every 5. The hand lead is used for soundings in rivers and harbours 20 fathoms. The small yacht need only have a 7-lb. lead weight and a 20-fathom leadline, or perhaps a lighter lead and shorter line for closer work inshore. The 20-fathom line is marked by leather at 2, 3 and 10 fathoms; white canvas or calico at 5 and 15 fathoms; red bunting at 7 and 17 fathoms; blue bunting at 13 fathoms and some knots of cord at the 20-fathom mark; all of which help the leadsman in the dark.

> *For England, when with favouring gale,*
> *Our gallant ship up Channel steered,*
> *And scudding, under easy sail,*
> *The high, blue western land appeared.*
> *To heave the lead the seaman sprung,*
> *And to the pilot cheerly sung*
> *"By the deep—Nine!"*

> *And bearing up to gain the port,*
> *Some well-known object kept in view,*
> *An abbey tower, a ruined fort,*
> *A beacon to the vessel true.*
> *While oft the lead the seaman flung,*
> *And to the pilot cheerly sung,*
> *"By the mark—Seven!"*

And as the much-loved shore drew near,
With transport we beheld the roof
Where dwelt a friend, or partner dear,
Of faith and love and matchless proof.
The lead once more the seaman flung,
And to the pilot cheerly sung,
     " Quarter less—Five !"

These are some verses from a song I am very fond of called "The Heaving of the Lead". You will notice that the leadsman says in one verse, "By the deep, nine!" The reason for this is that there is no mark there and he is only guessing it is 9 fathoms, it might easily be $8\frac{1}{2}$ or only 8, and the helmsman knows that this is a guess. But in the second verse he calls, "By the mark, seven!" and now the helmsman knows that he has the correct reading. The final call, "Quarter less five!" tells the helmsman again that the water is not exactly on a mark, so he could be a foot or two out with his call. When heaving the lead and calling out where there is no mark you call, "By the deep!" which tells the helmsman you are making the best guess you can. When you are on a mark you can call by it and when you are a quarter less you call a quarter less than whatever is the next mark. If the bottom of the lead is hollowed out and filled with a small piece of tallow, it will bring up shingle or sand or whatever is on the bottom, and as charts not only mark depths but also give an indication of the bottom, the navigator has a double guide.

All too few of us today care for and cherish our lead line, but it can be a great source of comfort and a guide for any ship. I have a set of charts dedicated to the Elder Brethren of Trinity House for 1824. There were very few lights around our coasts at that time and nearly all the navigation had to be done by the lead and line, so all the Channel and the Bay of Biscay is beautifully written up with a full description, not only of the depths but also of the nature of the bottom. All the old sea songs conjure up a picture of the leadsman and even in "Spanish Ladies", which has such a lovely tune, he is of vital importance to the song as far as seamen are concerned.

Today many a yacht has an echo-sounding device, a wonderful

instrument that will not only record the bottom but even a shoal of fish. But, wonderful as it is, every vessel should still have aboard and often use the lead and line; then her crew will become and remain fine seamen, and should any accident befall the echo-sounder they can heave the lead in a seamanlike manner.

Charts

Charts are of very great importance to the cruising man and to any seaman as they are the plan of his battlefield. The information to be gleaned from a chart is astonishing and, so carefully are they prepared that every detail required for navigation is recorded on them. Each one tells you when the survey was made and when the corrections have been added, so you always know the date and from this can judge its reliability. On every one there is a scale of feet and metres and a scale of miles with cables, there being 10 cables to a sea mile, which is a minute of latitude. There are the lines of longitude and latitude marked on the chart which positions it for any part of the globe; also there is the compass with its degrees from zero North right round the 360° to North again. And, inside this ring, which gives the true North, you have the magnetic North, to which your compass points, and you are also told exactly how much this magnetic variation decreases every year. And as, on this compass rose, the variation is given with its year, you can easily work out the variation for the year on which you are using the chart.

Often charts give a 20-fathom line, then a 10-fathom line and a glance at this will tell you immediately you come from the deeper soundings on to 20 fathoms and from the 20 on to 10 and then to 5: in effect, these lines show you the shape of the sea-bottom. Banks and rocks are all picked out; and all the different lights— lighthouses, lightships and lightbuoys—together with their flashes and colours. And while the land is not clearly defined, every conspicuous object is set out, as well as the height of the hills and the contours. So a careful study of the chart will give you a complete picture of the place you are going into, and a great deal of tidal information as well. The first thing is to discover what the soundings are in—generally they are marked in fathoms. There are 6 feet to a fathom and under 11 fathoms the depths are often given in fathoms and feet, while any underlined figure means that this is a bank or a rock which stands out of water by the amount underlined.

The lines of longitude on a chart run north and south and as each and every one of these lines meets, at the North and South Poles, the measurement in longitude varies from the Equator to the Poles; becoming smaller the farther you go north or south. But the lines of latitude are true and remain constant as they run east and west—from the Equator north and south—and each minute of latitude corresponds to one sea mile and therefore when you wish to measure on a chart you have only to put your dividers along the latitude at the side of the chart and you can see how many sea miles away one thing is from another.

Therefore, study your chart; make sure you understand everything on it and then start to get a picture of your next port by previous study. You will be surprised how easy it is to arrive in the haven where you would be.

Pilot Books

There are innumerable books that will help in navigation. For instance: *The Channel Pilot* will take you from the mouth of the Thames round to Land's End and the Scilly Isles—a distance of some 300 miles—and will give you information on the weather, currents, tides, signals, life-saving services, voyage communications, fuel, dockyards, pilotage and fisheries, as well as a complete description of the sea and land of this part of the world. Then there are the nautical almanacs which describe every light and buoy in detail, all the charges in the harbours for dock dues, and the heights and times of high water in every place of note in the world. Then there is the *Admiralty Light List* doing the same thing: and, a little book, *The Tides and Tidal Streams of the British Isles*. Later, when you start to use a sextant to take sights at the sun and stars, you will need nautical tables and books giving details of the sun and stars.

There are also books on sea cookery, for cooking afloat is more difficult than on shore because not only do you have to think farther ahead for provisions but your stove is often at an angle and the saucepans dancing a jig on it.

Many books have been written that will help the cruising man, dealing with weather, knots and splices and the Rule of the Road at Sea. And you have much to guide you on the charts themselves, not to mention books which tell you in words all that you can read on charts without them.

Binoculars

On shore you can use very powerful binoculars, as they can be arranged on a stand and held steady. You must, however, remember throughout your life that you can never get half a crown for sixpence, and that, with binoculars, what you gain in magnification you lose in the field and width of vision—and the greater the magnification the greater the eyestrain. Broadly speaking, you should never go to sea with binoculars of a power more than 6 or 7. Another thing to remember is that modern prisms are difficult on misty days; and whereas a straight telescope or a straight pair of old-fashioned glasses are quite good for looking through mist, ones with prisms, because of the reflected light, will not penetrate.

Sextant

The sextant is an instrument for measuring angles either up and down or from side to side, and is fairly simple to use. If you lay the sextant flat you can measure the angle your ship makes with two headlands and then plot this on the chart. But it is just as easy to lay these same angles off from your compass and then strike the two lines—one south-east and one south-west—off the chart and there is your position. At midday you can take a noon sight for latitude; you get out your sextant and with this measure the angle the sun is making with the skyline. You must watch the sun gradually rising up to its zenith, altering your sextant as it climbs. Once it has reached its meridian splendour you must not alter the sextant again—just check with it to make sure the sun is now descending—and that is your meridian altitude. This you subtract from 90°, so you get your angle and distance north or south of the sun in this latitude. Now from a nautical almanac you read exactly how much the sun is north or south of the Equator—its declination. If you are north and the declination is north you add declination, and you have your latitude north of the Equator. If your sight and the declination are the same, both north or both south, you add them together for latitude, but if one is north and one is south you subtract for latitude, a very simple calculation. This system was used by the early navigators before longitude was invented; if they were making for an island they would sail on to its latitude, and go east or west, keeping on this latitude until they picked up the island.

Thoughts

Do not put to sea in bad weather as you will get all you want of it without deliberately going out into it.

Try to avoid difficult harbours, especially in bad weather. Once you are in them they are even more difficult to get out of and if they have a bar it is so easy to get "baritis" and stay there a long time—you might even wreck your ship attempting to get in. Therefore it is better and safer to hold on and make for places such as the Solent or Falmouth and then, once you have made them, you can still have some sailing there, no matter what the weather continues to do. So try and avoid running for harbours on a lee shore; they are dangerous to enter because seas racing towards the land are tripped up by the rising ground as the water shallows and tumble and break as they become unstable, conditions under which your vessel can easily get completely out of control. So far better stay out and make for safer places.

Never put half-hitches on halyards or sheets; flying spray coming over will tighten them up so that they can never be undone.

Fog is one of the greatest dangers at sea, so you must have a jolly good bell that can be rung every three minutes at anchor and a loud foghorn that must be blown every minute when you are underway.

If you anchor on an open coast, and the wind is offshore, before turning in you must prepare for the wind swinging round and putting you on a lee shore. A working headsail should be ready to set in stops hanked on its stay, and the mainsail reefed: then, if the wind swings and you find that instead of the shore sheltering you it is now a danger, you are already prepared. You set your mainsail, hoist your jib in stops, heave the anchor up short, break the

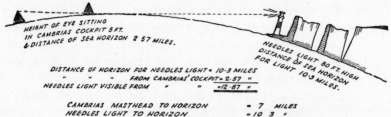

HEIGHT OF EYE SITTING IN CAMBRIAS COCKPIT 5 FT.
& DISTANCE OF SEA HORIZON 2 57 MILES.

NEEDLES LIGHT 80 FT. HIGH
DISTANCE OF SEA HORIZON
FOR LIGHT 10·3 MILES.

DISTANCE OF HORIZON FOR NEEDLES LIGHT = 10·3 MILES
"   "   "   FROM CAMBRIAS' COCKPIT = 2·57 "
NEEDLES LIGHT VISIBLE FROM   "   " =12·87 "

CAMBRIAS MASTHEAD TO HORIZON   = 7 MILES
NEEDLES LIGHT TO HORIZON   = 10 3 "
"   "   FROM CAMBRIAS MASTHEAD = 17·3 "

DISTANCE OF SEA HORIZON IN NAUTICAL MILES.

HEIGHT IN FEET	DISTANCE	HEIGHT IN FEET	DISTANCE
5	2·57	100	11·50
10	3·64	200	16·26
15	4·45	300	19·92
20	5·14	400	23·10
30	6·30	500	25·71
40	7·27	600	28·17
50	8·13	700	30·43
60	8·91	800	32·53
70	9·62	900	34·50
80	10·30	1000	36·37

jib out, heave up and break out and stow the anchor; then you are away with no confusion and in a minimum of time and effort.

If you are in a small boat your height of eye above the sea is generally 5 ft.—then the horizon is $2\frac{1}{2}$ miles away. It is therefore useless to look for buoys at a greater distance as they will be down under and out of sight. Lighthouses and lights which stand above the horizon generally have their heights given above sea-level, and upon their height depends their visibility and range. These are generally given for a height of eye of 15 ft. above sea-level at high water, so you must allow for tide and when you are this height your skyline is $4\frac{3}{4}$ miles away.

No matter how short the voyage we must be prepared for cuts and bruises, accidents and illnesses, so a medicine chest must be carried. I am a great believer in hydrogen peroxide for cuts as this fizzes out the impurities without harming the flesh, which then quickly heals. But everyone has a few favourite essentials in their medicine chest at home—these should be taken on the boat as well.

The fewer things we need the happier we are, so only take necessities and get along with these.

On every vessel there must be a place for everything and every-thing in its place. Once used, instruments, tools, ropes and tackles must be put back into their appointed places so that on a dark night any member of the crew can put a hand on his large marlin-spike or ball of twine without any trouble.

If you are moving about the deck and the only one on watch—as so often happens these days when one man can steer and handle a vessel—you should wear a safety-belt with 6 feet of rope and a clip. Then, if you are doing anything the least dangerous you can clip yourself on, secure also in the knowledge that if you tripped or fell or were washed overboard you would be held to the ship and could thus regain your place on deck.

Food

The stomach is the greatest nerve-centre in the body and has to cope with whatever we send down into it. If we send down soup that is too hot it has to work hard to cool it to the right tempera-ture for digestion. And if we send down food that is really cold it must warm it up before it can deal with it. This is all very well on land but at sea, with the boat heeling and toeing it to every wave as she dances over the sea, rolling over sideways then coming up-right as the squalls hit her, we should think of our tummy and give it the least possible work for the first few days at sea while it settles down to these new, tumbling conditions. The calmer our tummies the less prone they are to seasickness, so we must start to think about them some 24 hours before going to sea, and all the time we are at sea.

Greasy things such as fried bacon, fat pork and highly-spiced dishes—all things that cause our digestive organs to work to their maximum—must be avoided until we have been at sea for, say, three days. If I am in charge of a vessel I always have boiled fowls, enough to last for the first 48 hours at sea; I also have a ham, already boiled before we leave; and I take a great many eggs. Then, for the first breakfast at sea, we have a lovely slice of ham with poached or boiled eggs on top, a non-greasy breakfast. For the midday meal I have cold chicken and lettuce. None of these things calls for any great effort on the part of the cook and involve no greasy smells, only the boiling of pure water—and we have

given our digestions every chance and started them on the voyage
with every consideration. For the evening meal a grilled steak is
a good idea; and again there is no greasiness in the cooking. After
this we can settle down to cooking as usual as, if we are wise, we
started off in good weather. We must always remember that
heavy weather and gales of wind call for a great deal of strength
and courage, which can best be kept up by good hot food. Once
we have settled down aboard we can cook and eat soups and stews
and all sorts of wholesome food that is not too greasy, but we
should always avoid the frying-pan as much as possible as this
provides the greasy meals that put a strain on our digestion.

Water

We actually drink only three pints of water a day in the form of
tea and coffee and such things. For when cooking porridge, pota-
toes or cabbage there is just the exact amount of salt in sea water
that these require, so we can scoop up the sea for this, provided
we are clear of the land and its pollution of the sea by great towns.
Now, although our consumption of water is so small per day, we
cannot live long without it. The water supply on a vessel is therefore of the utmost importance: more important even, than food—
for you can always catch a fish whereas fresh water is very difficult
to find and the most important of all the stores.

The water-tanks, however small, should be divided into two or
more, and each one separate from the other so that we can draw
from any one in the galley and empty one tank completely, knowing full well that the others are there ready for use. Only by this
method can we continually have a fresh and clean supply of water,
for if it is all in one tank, or the tanks are connected together by a
levelling pipe, we can never, never have fresh supplies because,
never daring to let our tanks get completely empty, we are always
refilling them on top of some stale water. On shore every time we
flush a W.C. we throw away two or three gallons of perfectly pure
water, but afloat there is salt water pumped through for this purpose and fresh water is used only for drinking purposes.

Four of us once sailed the Atlantic quite happily on a 200-gallon
tank of water and had only used half of this when we arrived after
33 days at sea. Although highly important, the amount of fresh

water we require is small and it should be kept down under the cabin floor in the coolest part of the ship so that even in the tropics the heat does not worry or disturb it.

Some Early Voyages

Having decided on our vessel, large or small, we can start cruising and I know of no finer place to start from than Cowes. Here you are in the middle of the Solent Sea, with 15 miles of fairly sheltered waters westward, some 4 miles in width from Cowes to the Needles, and a similar distance in length and width to the eastward; with harbours for small vessels 4 miles apart. You can never be more than an hour from any harbour or more than 2 miles from the land. All around you throughout the summer are countless boats which would come to your assistance should you be in any danger through dismasting or torn sails. But although you have the land on either side, you have to contend with the tides, rocks, shoals and shingle banks, all calling for a high degree of sailing and seamanship. And, as the largest liners in the world, the *Queen Mary*, the *Queen Elizabeth* and the *United States of America*, as well as giant tankers, use these waters regularly, it is well buoyed: so you learn the international buoyage system from the very beginning. And although steam gives way to sail when it can, there are times when it cannot, and that is when these great ships are in narrow channels. A month or more of exploring all the lovely little rivers and harbours, such as Yarmouth, Lymington, Key Haven and Wootton, as well as Portsmouth and Southampton, will teach a man a great deal of navigation, sailing and seamanship, all with a certain amount of security. If he makes Cowes his sailing centre he has a 5-mile river to Newport which is fun to sail on when it blows really hard and the tide is high; also a good harbour with ship and yacht yards, engineering shops and rope works all around him, and tailors and outfitters who can supply every need.

We will make one or two imaginary sails from Cowes. We are off on a cruise in *Cambria*, this 24-ft. waterline, masthead cutter. It is the end of July and there is a smart south-westerly blowing about 25 m.p.h. We are on a mooring in Cowes Harbour inside the breakwater, and our plan is to sail up the Beaulieu river to Buckler's Hard. All cruises, long or short, are rather like a battle;

before you start you make a broad plan—the strategy—and this has minor changes as dictated by varying circumstances—the tactics: so we must make the outline plan before we start. Shakespeare makes Caesar say, "It boots us ill to resist both wind and tide". The tide is always with us and must be our first consideration. To make life simple I am going to eliminate Summer Time and work on Greenwich Time only, then you can add the one hour Summer Time, or the two hours Double Summer Time whichever one the Government puts on us. All nautical Almanacs give Greenwich Mean Time, and the longitude of the whole world is based on the observatory and meridian of Greenwich.

We should get under way for Beaulieu an hour and a half before high water, as this gives us every tidal advantage. The west-going stream turns and starts running down-Channel an hour and a half before high water at Cowes; so we will take a west-going tide to the mouth of Beaulieu River, which will push us up to windward. Once we are inside the river—which we shall reach in only about 20 minutes—we shall have another hour's fair tide running up the river to take us to our anchorage at Buckler's Hard.

We see that the mainsail is set taut on the boom and before hoisting it we decide to roll a reef in it, and set only the working jib as there is a strong south-wester pulling right up through the Solent channel from the Needles. We decide to set the working jib in stops on the forestay and attach the sheets, so we only have to pull on them to break out the jib at the right moment. In order to do this we stretch the luff of the working jib tight from the stem aft, then roll the jib up, tying tightly with some stopping cotton—a thin, white, easily broken cotton—having only one strand of this at the top where the sail is narrow and there is little sail to break loose; two or three strands as we come farther down the sail; and finally, four thicknesses at the clew so that all the time the strength of cotton is in proportion to the amount of sail. Once this is done we hank the luff of the jib on to the forestay with its piston hanks, and set it just exactly as taut as the forestay itself. We then attach the jibsheets, confident in the knowledge that the sail is set and only needs to be broken out. With our worm-rolling reefing gear we must be careful to pull the sail out taut at the after end when we are rolling the one reef in; then we hoist away on the main halyard and

at the Master Builders' House at Bucklers Hard. Then aboard and so to bed; well content.

After a quiet night we get under way at high water slack for our return sail down the Beaulieu River. As there is no tide we can set the one reef mainsail and the working jib, in stops, for we are swinging head to wind on our anchor. We heave the anchor chain up until our kedge warp is just above water, let it go from the anchor cable from the dinghy, and underrun it until we are over the kedge. Then we heave the kedge out clean off the mud; coil the warp down, and stow it all aboard, then we heave our anchor chain. Once we have the anchor on deck we break out the jib, sheeting it to starboard, swing our bow southward and away from the wind, and soon our boat has swung on her heel and—with the wind over her starboard quarter—is sailing down the Beaulieu River which winds soon to windward, so that we have to make one short tack on the southern stretch towards Needsoar Point. (We tow the dinghy, since we are staying inside the Solent.) Arriving there we steer eastwards between the mile long spit of land and the Solent, and reach along this stretch at a clinking pace with the first of the ebb under us and arrive at the entrance steering southwards close-hauled, keeping the leading marks in line.

We are soon out in the Solent with quite a jump of a sea, and spray flying over the decks. We continue close-hauled on the starboard tack standing right across the Solent to the Isle of Wight: then tacking to port, we start bucking into the steep Solent seas caused by a 3-knot tide against the wind. Past Newtown, the Solent Bank Buoy, and then we tack once more to starboard, driving southwards with a weather-going tide; and find ourselves being taken nicely past Yarmouth pier. Now with an easier tide we sail into the harbour, again keeping the leading marks in line.

In the harbour we shoot head to wind, and lower the jib with a run. By now the ebb is running out of the harbour so we have no difficulty in pointing head to wind and tide, and, stopping at our mooring-post, we make fast with the warp. We swiftly lower the mainsail, making a sternwarp fast to another mooring-post aft, and we are snug in one of the loveliest of harbours. Now we launch our dinghy: ashore there is the castle built by Henry VIII and in the old church a 20-minute sandglass used in the past by the

preacher for his sermon, and still sometimes used today. Both the
preacher and the congregation keep an eye on the sands running
out towards the end; it is a pity these ever went out of use. In the
old vestry is a statue of one of the greatest benefactors to women,
Louis XIV of France. It was he who invented the tall (Louis) heels
as he was a short chap and still wished to be impressive. This
statue was complete except for the face when it was captured by
Robert Holmes, a governor of the Isle of Wight. He brought the
statue and the sculptor home in the ship he had taken and made
the sculptor carve his, the governor's, own face. So here we have
Louis XIV with the face of Robert Holmes. We have a pleasant
dinner at the "George" which was the home of the Governor of
Yarmouth Castle, after which we row back aboard for the night.

The following day, 1½ hours before high water, we heave the
dinghy aboard (for we never, never tow a dinghy outside the
Wight), and get under way. Now we have a problem. We are
head to wind and are moored fore and aft, and the flood tide is still
running in the harbour against the wind. When wind and tide are
opposed it is always a difficult manœuvre to get under way or to
pick up a mooring, and we are moored between two posts. Our
easiest method of getting under way—for we are stern to the tide—
is to take the bow warp and pass this outside all the shrouds on the
port side, and pass the end through the ring on the stern mooring-
post. Now we have both ends back aboard and we let go our stern
warp and heave away on one part of the bow warp, the other being
made fast to a cleat on the port bow. This pulls our bow against
the tide, which is now swinging the stern round in a circle, and soon
we find our boat—still with no sails set—stem to tide and stern to
wind. As the bow is abreast the post we let go the short end made
fast to the cleat and haul our slip-rope aboard. There is enough
wind in the mast and rigging to hold her on the tide, so we break
out our jib, which is already set in stops, and quietly sail to leeward
out of the harbour. Directly we are clear of the bar and banks we
shoot her head to wind, and in smooth water in the lee of the Isle of
Wight we hoist our mainsail. Now we throw off on the port tack
and start sailing for Hurst Castle, also built by Henry VIII; we
begin beating our way down the Solent through the narrows of
Hurst and through the Needles Channel, keeping clear of the

Shingle Bank as the ebb tide sets across this and tends to sweep the boat on to this treacherous, moving bank of shingle. Finally, we make our last tack with the Needles lighthouse close abeam; and with the ebb tide pushing us to windward, we sail out between the Bridge and the South-West Shingle Buoys.

We now find that the wind which was pulling and following the coastline of the Isle of Wight is more southerly, as we are in the true Channel breeze, and we can almost sail west (magnetic) close-hauled on the port tack; so we can settle down for a long leg of 12 miles before having to tack and trim sheets. Behind is the lovely whiteness of Scratchells Bay and the Needles. Ahead are the white cliffs of Swanage with Old Harry and his wife; in ancient times the Needles and Swanage joined each other and the waters of Poole swept out past the Isle of Wight. On this quiet stretch, in under the lee of Swanage and Studland Bay, as well as enjoying the beauty of the coastline and watching the hills of Purbeck rising and rising, we can also let our mind wander back over the past history of the British Isles.

This tack takes us under the lee of Old Harry and to windward of the Poole Bar buoy. We make short tacks past Studland Anvil Point and the Dancing Ledges, close inshore to miss the race of St Albans Head, after which the coast runs away a bit and we can sail straight along it. Suddenly, in the white cliffs we see the opening into Lulworth Cove. There are two white ridges running out towards each other to form an entrance and to protect us from any sea running; and soon we have dropped anchor inside this lagoon, having taken a fair tide the whole way from Yarmouth to Lul-worth. Once again we run out our kedge with the dinghy, to moor ourselves safely. We take our working jib off its stay, stretch it out along the deck dry, stop it down and hank it once more to the jib-stay, ready for hoisting and breaking out. Then we loosen the mainsail to air, until an hour before sunset when we roll down one reef in it and we are all ready for a quick getaway in an emergency. We have a ramble ashore, and dinner, and after a quiet night we get our vessel shipshape for our return into the Solent.

We leave at low water so that we can take the whole of the east-going flood tide with us; and with the wind south-west we can lay out through the entrance close-hauled on the starboard tack.

Immediately we are outside we ease away our sheets, for with the wind abaft the beam we can sail along clear of the land and its out-lying rocks, close in alongside St Albans Head and clear of the Race. Then on past this iron-bound coast to Anvil Point until we can steer on the white cliffs of the Needles, gleaming out ahead. But we must point out to sea a quarter of a point or so as there is a strong indraught into all bays—for as the tide comes round head-lands it spreads out and fills the bays—and so we sail along quietly and gently until soon we are fairly close to the Needles.

The flood tide here now tends to set us into Scratchells Bay, and we must watch the land beyond the buoys to see which way we are being set by the tide so that by making the correct allowance we can steer a steady course in. Soon we are flying between the South-West Shingle Buoy and the Needles Bridge Buoy, both quite close together; the first marking the tail of the treacherous Shingle Bank which runs parallel with the Needles channel, and the other mark-ing the continuation of the Needles rocks out under the sea-bed. Once inside we are soon swirling away up towards the Narrows of Hurst and we have the row of Shingle bank buoys to warn us of the dangers to the north, and Warden Ledge Buoy—standing well out from the Island—to keep us off the Warden Ledge. Soon we boil in through the Narrows of Hurst and on towards Cowes, and as we arrive we sharpen in towards the land, hauling in our sheets, for the wind will tend to pull out of the river.

As it is now just on high water we can, if we have a mooring, go in and pick it up. If we have none we can enter the fairway, and a quarter of a mile inside on the starboard hand we can moor up, fore and aft to the posts. With a sailing boat it is easiest and best to luff into the wind, put a warp on the bow-post and let her lay, head to wind, while we stow our mainsail. Immediately this is done, run out a warp to the post farther aft. In summertime it is right to lay with your bow in the river, as if it comes on to rain it will come out of the south-west. Then, instead of driving into the cabin, the rain will go flying past and you can keep the cabin door open aft to let in air and allow people to come in and out without hindrance. But if you are moored here after August, it is best to turn your ship round and put her head out when you have stowed your sails: then take your anchor chain round the post with both ends aboard, so that you have something strong to hold you against the north-easter which often comes up in the autumn. Moored in this way you can feel secure and contented in the knowledge that your chain will hold, and that if anything untoward happens and you have to get out, you just let your warps go aft, set your sails and haul up close to your mooring-post. Then, at the right moment, let go the end of your chain and haul it aboard, afterwards breaking out your jib which you have, as usual, set in stops. You can be off on the port tack fairly easily, after having lain all this time head-to wind and sea.

After a few more sails such as this—visiting all the little harbours in the Solent, and the various bays—you will have learnt how to handle your ship at sea and in harbour; on her anchor; on a mooring; and moored to posts. So your apprenticeship is well advanced and you can now consider going across Channel and visiting various French ports. Seamanship and seamanlike practices are the same all over the world even if the language is different; so though on arrival in a foreign port you may think that the chap is suffering from lockjaw, as you cannot understand what he says, if he is pointing to something it is up to you to decide whether it is a hidden rock, a place to moor, or if it means that you are standing into danger. And having full control of your little ship and having learnt a lot of seamanship, you will find that, whichever it is, you can decide quite easily on the right course of action. So now you have the Seven Seas before you, all for your delight.

But you must at all times remember that the power of the sea is greater than anything else on this earth; and that although many fleets have sailed over it, not one has conquered or harnessed it, and no one ever will. Remember, too, that like fire, the sea is a good friend but a bad master; so you must never, never allow yourself to get into the position where the sea takes control.